But for the Grace of God

Grace of God

An Exposition of the Canons of Dort

Cornelis P. Venema

Reformed
Fellowship Inc.
www.reformedfellowship.net

Reformed Fellowship, Inc., is a religious and strictly nonprofit organization composed of a group of Christian believers who hold to the biblical Reformed faith. Its purpose is to advocate and propagate this faith, to nurture those who seek to live in obedience to it, to give sharpened expression to it, to stimulate the doctrinal sensitivities of those who profess it, to promote the spiritual welfare and purity of the Reformed churches, and to encourage Christian action.

Requests for permission to quote from this book should be directed to Editor, *Reformed Fellowship, Inc. (877) 532–8510 president@reformedfellowship.net.*

All scripture quotations, unless otherwise indicated, are taken from the Holy Bible, New International Version®, NIV®. Copyright © 1973, 1978, 1984 by Biblica, Inc.™ Used by permission of Zondervan. All rights reserved worldwide. www.zondervan.com

Book Design by Jeff Steenholdt & Erika De Vries

Printed in the United States of America

ISBN 978-0-9653981-2-1

On the cover
Een vergadering van de Nationale Synode te Dordrecht, 1619
(1910–1911)
Gerard van Hove

To my parents, Richard and Carrie Venema,
from whom I first learned of God's amazing grace.

Contents

Preface

We live in a period of history in which there is little appreciation for inheritances received from the past. The church of Jesus Christ has increasingly forgotten its indebtedness for what she has received from the Lord in the confessions of the church.

This little study of a great confession of the Reformed churches, the Canons of Dort, is offered in the hope that it will reacquaint some believers with one of these inheritances. Many believers who sing lustily John Newton's "Amazing Grace" or the familiar hymn, "I Love to Tell the Story," need to understand in greater depth and fullness the biblical teaching that salvation is by grace alone through Christ alone. There is no single Christian confession that sings more vigorously of God's grace in Christ toward His people than the Canons of Dort.

The chapters of this study were originally written for a monthly column in *The Outlook*, a bi-monthly periodical dedicated to the propagation and defense of the Reformed faith. They have been only slightly modified for publication in this study. To enhance the usefulness of these chapters as a stimulus to further study and reflection, "Questions for Discussion" have been added at the conclusion of each chapter. In some instances, a few selected readings are also recommended for further study.

Scripture references throughout are taken from the New American Standard Version. All references to the Canons of Dort are taken from a 1986 translation of the Christian Reformed Church. This new translation of the Canons of Dort is printed with permission as an appendix, so that the reader can consult the full text of the confession whenever needed.

This study is offered with the hope that it will contribute to a renewed appreciation for the gospel of grace, as this is confessed in the confession known as the Canons of Dort. May a renewed acquaintance with this confession contribute to our telling the story—*but for the grace of God!*

Chapter One

An Introduction

to the Canons of Dort

One of the great treasures of the Reformed churches is the confession of faith known as the Canons of Dort. Written in reply to the unbiblical teachings of Jacobus Arminius and the Remonstrants, this confession beautifully sets forth the teaching of the Word of God that believers are saved by grace alone, from first to last. According to the Canons of Dort, salvation—from its conception in the eternal counsel of God the Father, to its provision in the person and work of God the Son (the Mediator), to its application by God the Holy Spirit through the gospel—is sovereignly authored and accomplished by the triune God. Following the example of the apostle Paul, the Canons of Dort give praise to God alone for the election of His people to salvation: "For from Him and through him and to Him are all things. To Him be the glory forever. Amen" (Rom. 11:36).

Though many Reformed Christians in our day are still familiar with the Canons of Dort, this confession is not nearly as well known as it should be. Even among Reformed believers there are many who are either uninformed or misinformed about the Canons' summary of the biblical teaching of election. Sadly, though often unread and unstudied, the Canons are frequently caricatured and misrepresented by those unwilling to submit to the scriptural teaching they summarize. Since so much of contemporary evangelicalism in North America subscribes to a basically Arminian view of salvation, there are many Reformed believers whose understanding of the doctrine of salvation has been compromised or distorted by Arminian views.

Moreover, among the mainline Protestant denominations there is open embarrassment over many aspects of biblical teaching, and especially over the doctrine of predestination. A recent statement, for example, of a theological commission of representatives of five such mainline churches, reveals the difficulty these denominations have with the doctrine of election. This statement concluded that, rather than being divided over the doctrine, the churches are embarrassed at any form of predestinarian teaching and no longer consider it part of their theological commitment.[1] This statement well reflects the general approach within mainline Protestantism to the subject of predestination and election: the doctrine is either unknown or the object of benign neglect, even embarrassment.

Consequently, there is a pressing need today for Reformed Christians to reacquaint themselves with the Canons of Dort. To contribute to such a reacquaintance, I hope in this and several subsequent chapters to provide a brief summary of the teaching of this great confession of faith. Before directly considering the teaching of the Canons, however, I will briefly sketch in this chapter the background and history that led up to the meeting of the Synod of Dort in 1618–19. Only in this way is it possible to appreciate fully the positive, biblical affirmations of the Canons and the errors that the Reformed fathers rejected at this Synod.

The Historical Occasion for the Synod of Dort

Though a complete recounting of the history that preceded the calling of a synod of the Reformed churches at Dordrecht, the

---

1. This commission report represents the culmination of a series of Lutheran-Reformed talks going back to 1962. The churches represented are: the Evangelical Lutheran Church in America, the Presbyterian Church (U.S.A.), the United Church of Christ, and the Reformed Church in America. Not only does the commission report seriously misrepresent the historic, biblical teaching of election, but it also betrays the extent to which these denominations have largely abandoned their confessional heritage.

Netherlands, in 1618 would require more attention than we can give it here, there are some aspects of the history prior to this synod that are of special importance.

Not long after the Reformed faith took root and prospered in the Netherlands in the middle of the sixteenth century (c. 1544), a serious controversy arose concerning the preaching and teaching of Jacobus Arminius (1560–1609). Arminius, a brilliant student of Theodore Beza, Calvin's successor in Geneva, Switzerland, initiated the controversy by preaching a series of sermons on Paul's epistle to the Romans. In these sermons Arminius proposed a number of controversial points: that death would have been inevitable, even were Adam to have remained obedient; that Romans 7 is a description of Paul in his unregenerate state; that man retains, even after the fall, a free will by which to obey or disobey the demands of the gospel; and that the civil government has authority over the church.[2]

However, the most important aspect of Arminius's position became evident in his attack on the Reformed doctrine of predestination. Arminius betrayed his position when he expressed serious reservations concerning Article 16 of the Belgic Confession. This Article, entitled "Eternal Election," briefly summarized the biblical teaching of unconditional election:

> We believe that, all the posterity of Adam being thus fallen into perdition and ruin by the sin of our first parents, God then did manifest Himself such as He is; that is to say, merciful and just: *merciful*, since He delivers and preserves from this perdition all whom He in His eternal and unchangeable counsel of mere goodness has elected in Christ Jesus our Lord, without any respect to their works; *just*, in leaving others in the fall and perdition wherein they have involved themselves.

Against this article's insistence on unconditional election, Arminius argued that election to salvation is based on the

---

2. Arminius was not only a pastor of the Reformed churches, but he was also an influential theologian at the University of Leiden.

divine foreknowledge of faith; God elected to save His people, not sovereignly and graciously, but on the condition of foreseen faith.

Arminius's preaching and teaching became the eye of a subsequent storm of controversy that was provoked among the Reformed churches in the Netherlands. During this period the churches were racked with controversy, and two parties emerged: a party favoring the position of Arminius and a party opposing his position. Two important events also occurred, preparing the way for the calling of the Synod of Dort in 1618.

After Arminius's death in 1609, the Arminian party in the Dutch Reformed churches prepared a summary statement of their position. On January 14, 1610, more than forty representatives who championed Arminius's views gathered in Gouda. These representatives drew up a Remonstrance or petition in which their case was set forth and defended. After complaining that their cause had been misrepresented by their opponents and arguing that the state had authority over the affairs of the church, this Remonstrance presented the Arminian position in a series of five articles.[3] The Remonstrants hoped that this statement would be presented for approval by the civil authorities, thereby answering the

---

3. Hence this Remonstrance is often termed the "Five Arminian Articles" (Latin: *Articuli Arminiani sive Remonstrantia*). These "five" articles became the organizing pattern for the discussions and debates that ensued, including the five "heads of doctrine" of the Canons of Dort. Hence the "five points of Calvinism," commonly so-called, are really five "counter-points" to the errors of the Arminians or Remonstrants. Today, they are often known by the acronym, "TULIP." Though this acronym changes the order of the five points, it is a useful help to remember the main contents of this confession: Total depravity, Unconditional election, Limited atonement, Irresistible grace, and the Perseverance of the saints.

charge that their doctrine was in conflict with Scripture and the Reformed confessions.[4]

Shortly after this Remonstrance was prepared, the States of Holland made arrangements for a meeting between representatives of the Arminian or Remonstrant and the anti-Arminian parties. This meeting took place from March 10, 1611, until May 20, 1611, and was the occasion for the preparation of a reply to the Remonstrance of the Arminians. This reply of the Reformed or Calvinist defenders of the faith was termed the Counter Remonstrance of 1611. In this reply the main lines of the later, more expansive statement of the Canons of Dort were anticipated.

Finally, when the debate between Arminian/Remonstrant and anti-Arminian/Counter Remonstrant showed no signs of abating in the Netherlands, the States-General of the Republic of the Netherlands called a national synod to settle the dispute. The express purpose of this synod, to be held in 1618 in Dordrecht, was to judge whether the position of the Remonstrants was in harmony with the Word of God and the Reformed Confessions, particularly Article XVI of the Belgic Confession. Though officially a synod of the Reformed churches of the Netherlands, the synod had in addition twenty-six delegates from eight foreign countries.

On the basis of its deliberations, the Synod of Dort judged the five articles of the Remonstrants to be contrary to the Word of God and the confession of the Reformed churches. Against the Arminian teachings of election based on foreseen faith, human depravity, resistible grace, and the possibility of a lapse from grace, the Canons set forth the Reformed teachings of unconditional election, limited atonement, total depravity, irresistible grace, and the perseverance of the saints. In form,

---

4. One interesting feature of the Arminian controversy in the Netherlands was the role of the state in the affairs of the church. Not only did the Arminian "party" solicit the aid of the civil authorities in promoting their views, but the Synod of Dort was also called in 1618 by the States-General of the United Republic of the Netherlands.

the Canons were structured to answer to the five points of the Remonstrance. On each major head of doctrine, the Canons first present a positive statement of the scriptural teaching, and then conclude with a rejection of the corresponding Arminian error.

The Teaching of Arminius and the Remonstrants

From this brief sketch of the history leading up to the calling of the Synod of Dort in 1618, it becomes apparent that the Reformed churches of the Netherlands, indeed the Reformed churches internationally, faced at this time their greatest crisis since the early days of the Reformation. At stake was the Reformed confession of the sovereign grace of God in salvation.

To appreciate the nature and extent of this crisis, a summary of the distinctives of the Arminian or Remonstrant doctrine of grace is required. In summarizing the Arminian teaching, I will follow the pattern of "five articles" established by the Arminians in 1610.

The First Article: Conditional Election

The first and perhaps most important article of the Arminian/ Remonstrant position affirmed the teaching of "conditional" election. According to the Arminian position, God elected before the foundation of the world to save those who He foresaw would respond to the gospel call. Election therefore was determined by or conditioned on what man would do with the gospel. God does not give faith to the elect whom He is pleased to save. Rather, God foresees those who will believe and repent of their own free will at the preaching of the gospel and chooses to save them on the basis of this foreseen faith. Election is, therefore, neither sovereign nor unmerited in the strict sense of these terms. Similarly, those whom God reprobates or chooses not to save, He reprobates on the basis of foreseen unbelief. Hence, sinful man's choice to believe in Christ, not God's choice to give the sinner to Christ, becomes the ultimate cause of the salvation of the believer.

The Second Article: Universal Atonement

In the second article of the Arminian/Remonstrant position, it is said that Christ "died for all men and for every man," although only those who believe in Him as He is presented in the gospel will be saved. The atoning work of Christ made it possible for everyone to be saved, without actually securing the salvation of anyone. By virtue of Christ's atoning work, it becomes possible for God to forgive sinners on the condition that they believe. But Christ's atoning work does not actually "remove" anyone's sins or provide salvation for a particular people, namely, those whom the Father would give to Him or for whom He offered Himself a sacrifice. Christ's work of atonement makes salvation possible and available to all men without distinction, but without the certainty of having atoned for anyone in particular.

The Third Article: Human Depravity

When the framers of the Canons of Dort addressed the third article of the Arminian/Remonstrant view, which dealt with the extent of human depravity or sinfulness, they combined their treatment of human depravity with their treatment of efficacious or irresistible grace. In the opinion of the Remonstrants, fallen sinners do not have the freedom to will any saving good without the prior work of God's grace through the gospel. On this point there was no substantial disagreement between the Remonstrants and the authors of the Canons. However, consistent with the Arminian insistence that election is based on foreseen faith, and that Christ's atoning work becomes effective only through the free choice of some to believe the gospel, the Arminian/Remonstrant position also maintained that human depravity is mitigated through the grace that comes to all who are called to faith through the gospel. While acknowledging that human nature has been seriously affected by the fall, the Arminian position insists that fallen human nature is no longer completely helpless due to a work of grace that is common to all who hear the gospel. There is a general or common gracious working of God in the hearts of sinful men, short of granting salvation, which enables them to repent and believe. This enabling grace permits all men to cooperate or not cooperate with the gospel call to faith and repentance.[5] The sinner retains a free will, and his eternal destiny depends on the way he uses it. Though the lost sinner needs the Holy Spirit's assistance, he does not need to be regenerated by the Spirit before he can believe. Indeed, the new birth is preceded by man's act of faith; it is not the source of faith. Faith is man's contribution, his "good work" or accomplishment, which comes before the work of the Spirit in regeneration.

The Fourth Article: Resistible Grace

In the fourth article the Arminian party taught that the Holy Spirit calls inwardly all who are called through the gospel. The Holy Spirit does all He is able to bring every sinner to salvation, but this working of the Spirit may be successfully resisted. Because man is free and faith must precede and make possible the new birth, the Spirit cannot regenerate the sinner until he believes. Accordingly, the application by the Spirit of Christ's work to the sinner is limited and defined by the sinner's willingness to cooperate. The Holy Spirit can only draw through the gospel those who allow Him to have His way. God's grace is not irresistible, but resistible; it is not invincible, but vincible.

---

5. It should be noted that the Arminian position is not pure Pelagianism. Pelagianism teaches that man is able, *without any prior working of the grace of God*, to obey the law of God and thereby earn salvation. The Arminian position, like that of classical Roman Catholicism, tends toward semi-Pelagianism. It teaches that, with a prior and general working of the grace of God, all men are *enabled* to believe or not believe. However, the decisive step, the step that determines whether one is saved, belongs to the sinner, not God. To paraphrase a well-known comment of St. Augustine, in this position God does not "make" men elect, but "finds" men elect. God is finally left a hapless bystander or spectator who must wait for sinful man to make the all-important decision to be saved.

The Fifth Article: Perseverance of the Saints

The last article of the Arminian party was addressed to the question whether believers are preserved in the state of grace by the Holy Spirit. Here the Arminian/Remonstrant position was initially uncertain. In the early period of the controversy, some taught that it was possible for those who believe and are saved to be lost subsequently, should they fail to persevere in faith and obedience; others taught that believers are eternally secure in Christ, that once a believer was regenerated he could no longer be lost.[6] However, by the time the Synod of Dort was held in 1618, the Arminian party had repudiated the teaching that the saints persevere or are preserved in a state of grace by the work of the Spirit.

The Gospel at Stake, Then and Now

The Canons of Dort, though addressed to the particular teachings of Arminius in the historical setting of the post-Reformation debate in the Reformed churches of the Netherlands, continue to express the living faith of Reformed churches to this day. Nothing less than the heart of the gospel was at stake then. Nothing less than the heart of the gospel remains just as much at stake today. In whatever dress or style it may present itself, the Arminian teaching remains a constant threat and temptation to the churches' confession of salvation by grace alone. Consequently, the Canons of Dort continue to be needed as an answer and protection against this threat.

Two great themes of the gospel were threatened by the Arminian teaching. The first theme is the singular honor and

---

6. The fifth article of The Remonstrance of 1610 read: "But whether they can through negligence fall away from the first principle of their life in Christ, again embrace the present world, depart from the pure doctrine once give to them, lose the good conscience, and neglect grace, must first be more carefully determined from the Holy Scriptures before we shall be able to teach this with the full persuasion of our heart" (quoted in *Crisis in the Reformed Churches: Essays in Commemoration of the Great Synod of Dort, 1618–1619*, ed. by P. Y. De Jong [Grand Rapids: Reformed Fellowship, Inc., 1968, 2008], p. 245).

glory of God in the salvation of His people. The Arminian doctrine of salvation always divides between God and the sinner what belongs solely to God. Rather than testifying to and defending the biblical teaching that our salvation is wholly of grace, the Arminian teaching ascribes to the sinner a part, indeed the decisive part, in saving himself.[7]

But this compromising of the sovereign grace of God comes at a very high price. For it effectively undermines a second theme of the gospel, namely, the believer's assurance and security in the invincible grace of God. Because Arminian teaching places salvation in the hands of the lost sinner, it is unable to affirm that God's saving purpose for His people will be infallibly accomplished. If salvation depends on the free choice of the sinner (and a free choice in which the sinner must himself persevere), if it is not sovereignly designed, graciously secured, and irresistibly applied by God Himself, then the sinner's salvation hangs by the weakest of threads.

The framers of the Canons of Dort understood this. Therefore, they bequeathed to the Reformed churches the treasure of this confession. May Reformed believers today prove to understand it as well, cherishing this confession as a landmark of their inheritance in the faith.

Recommended Reading:

De Jong, Peter Y., ed. *Crisis in the Reformed Churches: Essays in Commemoration of the Great Synod of Dort, 1618–1619*. Grand Rapids: Reformed Fellowship, Inc., 1968, 2008.

Steele, David N., & Thomas, Curtis C., eds. *The Five Points of Calvinism: Defined, Defended, Documented*. Phillipsburg, NJ: Presbyterian & Reformed Publishing Co., 1963.

---

7. It should be noted that this is the inevitable consequence of the Arminian *formulation* of the doctrine of salvation. However, as the Dutch theologian, Herman Bavinck, is reported to have remarked, "All believers, when they confess their faith in prayer to God, are Reformed in acknowledging that their salvation is wholly of grace."

Questions for Discussion

1. Why do Reformed churches have doctrinal standards like the Canons of Dort? Why are they sometimes called "forms of unity"?

2. Is doctrinal controversy, like that which surrounded the Synod of Dort, a good thing? How are doctrinal differences to be settled?

3. Do you think the Arminian view of election is prevalent in many churches today? Explain.

4. Sometimes the teaching of the Canons of Dort is described as the "five points of Calvinism." Are these five points an adequate summary of Calvinism or the Reformed faith? Explain your answer in terms of what you know about the history leading up to the calling of the Synod of Dort in 1618.

Chapter Two

Unconditional Election

The First Main Point of Doctrine

In the preceding chapter, outlining the background to the calling of the Synod of Dort in 1618 and introducing the Canons of Dort, I noted that the Canons were written expressly to reply to the "five articles" of the Remonstrance of 1610. They were written to affirm the scriptural teaching of election and to reject the errors of the Arminian party in the Reformed churches of the Netherlands. This accounts for the way the Canons are structured. They address in succession the "five articles" of the Arminians or the Remonstrants, first presenting a positive statement of the scriptural teaching, and then rejecting the errors of the Arminians.

Consequently, the first main point of doctrine set forth in the Canons, written in reply to the first article of the Remonstrance of 1610, deals with the subject of "unconditional election." Whereas the Remonstrant/Arminian position taught that God's election to save His people was based on foreseen faith, the Canons affirm that God's election to save His people is based solely on His sovereign grace and mercy.

Since I will be following the order of the Canons in this and subsequent chapters, I will begin by summarizing the position of the Canons on the scriptural teaching of unconditional election. After setting forth this position, I will consider the scriptural basis for the Canons' teaching. In conclusion, two matters that have been much discussed in the history of the Reformed churches will be addressed briefly—the doctrine of reprobation and the preaching of the gospel of election.

The Position of the Canons

The title given to the "first main point of doctrine" by the Synod of Dort reads as follows: "Divine Election and Reprobation: The judgment concerning divine predestination which the synod declares to be in agreement with the Word of God and accepted till now in the Reformed Churches, set forth in several articles." This title clearly shows that the framers of the Canons wanted to articulate the historic view of unconditional election, long held in the Reformed churches, and to oppose the innovations of the Arminians.

After noting in the opening articles of the confession that "all people have sinned in Adam and have come under the sentence of the curse and eternal death" (Article 1),[1] that God has manifested His love in the sending of His only-begotten Son (Article 2), and that God's anger continues to rest on those who

---

1. In the history of the Reformed churches, a long debate has been carried on between those who take an "infralapsarian" and a "supralapsarian" position on the order of God's eternal decree. According to the "supralapsarian" (lit. "before the fall") position, the election and reprobation of individuals are logically prior to or before the divine decree to create the world and to permit the fall. In this position, the "first" purpose of God is the revelation of His glory in the salvation of the elect and the damnation of the reprobate; the purpose of God in creation and the fall are "secondary" as "means" to effect this primary purpose. According to the "infralapsarian" (lit. "after the fall") position, the order of God's decree parallels the historical order of creation, fall and redemption. This "infralapsarian" position teaches that God's decree to create the world and to permit the fall is prior to the decree to save the elect. Though proponents of both of these positions have argued vigorously that their position is the position of the Reformed confessions, particularly the Canons of Dort, I would insist that these two positions represent divergent theological viewpoints within a common confessional bond. In my judgment, it is a mistake to make either position a test of orthodoxy. What is perfectly clear is that the Canons, echoing Scripture, view God's free decision from all eternity to save His people in Christ on the assumption of man's fallen condition and misery.

do not believe the gospel of Jesus Christ (Article 3), the Canons raise directly the crucial question—how is it that some believe in Christ and are saved, while others continue in their sin and unbelief? Or, to put the question differently, the confession asks, why do some believe and repent at the preaching of the gospel, but others remain in their sins and under the just condemnation of God?

To this question—why are some men saved through the gospel, while others perish in unbelief?—the Canons answer: some are saved because God elects to save them and give them faith through the preaching of the gospel; others are not saved because God leaves them in their sin and chooses not to give them faith. Before the foundation of the world, God sovereignly chose, out of mere grace and mercy, certain individuals from among the fallen human race to be the recipients of His favor and grace.

In order to capture the heart of the Canons' teaching in this first main point of doctrine, the following affirmations are especially important:

> The fact that some receive from God the gift of faith within time, and that others do not, stems from [God's] eternal decision. For *all his works are known to God from eternity* (Acts 15:18; Eph. 1:11). In accordance with this decision he graciously softens the hearts, however hard, of his chosen ones and inclines them to believe, but by his just judgment he leaves in their wickedness and hardness of heart those who have not been chosen. And in this especially is disclosed to us his act— unfathomable, and as merciful as it is just—of distinguishing between people equally lost (Article 6).

> Election is God's unchangeable purpose by which he did the following: Before the foundation of the world, by sheer grace, according to the good pleasure of his will, he chose in Christ to salvation a definite number of particular people out of the entire human race, which

had fallen by its own fault from its original innocence into sin and ruin. Those chosen were neither better nor more deserving than the others, but lay with them in the common misery. He did this in Christ, whom he also appointed from eternity to be the mediator, the head of all those chosen, and the foundation of their salvation (Article 7).

This sovereign and gracious purpose of God in the election of His people is the source and basis of faith, and cannot therefore be based on faith. As the confession adds in Article 8,

This same election took place, not *on the basis of* foreseen faith, of the obedience of faith, of holiness, or of any other good quality and disposition, as though it were based on a prerequisite cause or condition in the person to be chosen, but rather *for the purpose of* faith, of the obedience of faith, of holiness, and so on.

Thus, the single basis of God's election is His good pleasure to save His people (Article 10). In His sovereign grace and mercy, the Father has been pleased to save a special people for the sake of His Son. This alone is the foundation on which our salvation is built.

After having articulated the scriptural teaching of unconditional election, the Canons further note that this sovereign and gracious election of a particular number of persons to salvation means that some sinners have been "passed by" and "left" in their sins.

Moreover, Holy Scripture especially highlights this eternal and undeserved grace of our election and brings it out more clearly for us, in that it further bears witness that not all people have been chosen but that some have not been chosen or have been passed by in God's eternal election—those, that is, concerning whom God, on the basis of the entirely free, most just, irreproachable, and unchangeable good pleasure, made the following decision:

to leave them in the common misery into which, by their own fault, they have plunged themselves; not to grant them saving faith and the grace of conversion; but finally to condemn and eternally punish them (having been left in their own ways and under his just judgment), not only for their unbelief but also for all their other sins, in order to display his justice. And this is the decision of reprobation, which does not at all make God the author of sin (a blasphemous thought!) but rather its fearful, irreproachable, just judge and avenger (Article 15).

In summary, then, this is the teaching of the Canons on unconditional election: before the foundation of the world, God was pleased to elect His people to salvation from among the fallen human race, leaving others in their sin and misery. Faith is, accordingly, not the basis or foundation of the salvation of the elect; faith is rather the fruit of God's gracious purpose to save His people and to produce such faith through the gospel. Though the Canons proceed in subsequent articles to consider several further aspects of God's saving purpose and work—including the redeeming and atoning work of the Son and the renewing work of the Spirit through the gospel—they properly insist that God's purpose of election is the wellspring and fountain whence flow all of the redemptive works of the triune God in history. "For from Him and through Him and to Him are all things. To Him be the glory forever. Amen" (Rom. 11:36).

The Scriptural Support for This Position

In Reformed churches, the authority of the confessions is always subordinate to and derived from the Scriptures. The confessions are understood to be summaries of the teachings of the written Word of God. They are therefore always subject to the test of Scripture—do they indeed faithfully set forth what the Word of God teaches?

This question holds as well, therefore, for the Canons of Dort and their statement of the doctrine of unconditional election—is this position biblical?

Rather than attempt to address all of the biblical passages that support the position of the Canons, it will be enough to cite only some of those passages explicitly appealed to in the confession itself.[2]

One of the first passages cited in this part of the Canons is Ephesians 1:4–6:

> He [the God and Father of our Lord Jesus Christ] chose us in Him [Christ] before the foundation of the world, that we should be holy and blameless before Him. In love He predestined us to adoption as sons through Jesus Christ to Himself, according to the kind intention of His will, to the praise of the glory of His grace, which he freely bestowed on us in the Beloved.

In this passage, the apostle Paul, within the setting of a doxology of blessing and praise to the God and Father of our Lord Jesus Christ, confesses that the believing children of God in Ephesus were the beneficiaries of God's electing love in Christ. Among the many blessings that were theirs in Christ—adoption, the forgiveness of sins, holiness, redemption—this blessing deserves pride of place. Indeed, all of these blessings flow from God's gracious election. Before the foundation of the world, God the Father set His eye on His own people in and for the sake of His Son. From all eternity He elected and predestined in love a peculiar people for His own possession. This purpose of election, far from being based on a foreseen faith or holiness, is an election "unto" faith and holiness (v. 4). Because this electing purpose is founded solely on the good pleasure of God, it is also solely

---

2. For a more complete and comprehensive treatment of the scriptural basis for the Canons' teaching, see: Steele, David N., & Thomas, Curtis, C., eds., *The Five Points of Calvinism: Defined, Defended, Documented* (New Jersey: Presbyterian & Reformed Publishing Co., 1963), pp. 30–38.

"unto the praise of the glory of His grace" (v. 6). In addition to this beautiful statement of God's unconditional election of His own people in Christ, the Canons also appeal to the affirmation of Romans 8:30: "those whom [God] predestined, these He also called; and those whom He called, these He also justified; and those whom He justified, these He also glorified." This affirmation occurs within the context of the apostle's declaration that "God causes all things to work together for good to those who love God, to those who are called according to His purpose" (Rom. 8:28). Since God has predestined to save His people in Christ, all those who have been "called according to His purpose" may be fully confident that God will invincibly achieve what He has purposed. So certain of accomplishment is God's purpose, according to this passage, that the calling, justification and glorification of those whom God has predestined is virtually assured.[3]

When the Canons proceed to show from Scripture that this electing purpose of God is solely founded on His good pleasure, and not on anything in the believer, they appeal particularly to Romans 9:11–13. In this passage, the apostle Paul answers the question, why are some and not others of those who belong to "Israel" saved? After having noted in Romans 9:1–5 that many of the children of Israel "according to the flesh" had rejected Christ, the apostle raises the question, has the "word of God . . . failed" (v. 6)? His answer, in brief, is: "certainly not!" Throughout the history of God's dealings with His people, God has been accomplishing His "purpose according to election," saving those whom He wills and not saving others.

To illustrate the manner in which God has been working out His electing purpose, the apostle cites the example of Jacob

---

3. It is striking that, in the sequence of verbs in Rom. 8:30 ("predestined," "called," "justified," "glorified"), all are in the past tense, signifying a series of specific acts that already have been accomplished. Such is the unbroken link between these aspects of what God has purposed to accomplish for those called according to His purpose that even their glorification (something yet to be accomplished at the coming of Christ) is, as it were, already done.

and Esau: "For though the twins were not yet born, and had not done anything good or bad, in order that God's purpose according to His choice [election] might stand, not because of works, but because of Him who calls, it was said to her, 'The older will serve the younger.' Just as it is written, 'Jacob I loved, but Esau I hated'" (Rom. 9:11–13). In the context of the argument in Romans 9–11, the point the apostle wishes to make in these verses is clear. The one is saved and the other is lost, not because the one is worthy and the other unworthy, not because the one has done good and the other evil, but merely because of God's gracious and electing choice.

There are several other passages cited by the Canons in support of their confession of unconditional election. Among them are the following: Ephesians 2:8, "For by grace you have been saved through faith; and that not of yourselves, it is the gift of God"; Philippians 1:29, "For to you it has been granted for Christ's sake, not only to believe in Him, but also to suffer for His sake"; Eph. 1:11, "also we have obtained an inheritance, having been predestined according to His purpose who works all things after the counsel of His will"; Acts 13:48, "And when the Gentiles heard this [Paul and Barnabas's preaching concerning God's purpose to save the Gentiles], they began rejoicing and glorifying the word of the Lord; and as many as had been appointed to eternal life believed"; John 17:6, "I [Jesus] manifested Thy name to the men whom Thou gavest Me out of the world; Thine they were, and Thou gavest them to Me, and they have kept Thy Word"; and 2 Tim. 1:9, "who [God] has saved us, and called us with a holy calling, not according to our works, but according to His own purpose and grace which was granted us in Christ Jesus from all eternity."

This sampling of passages cited in the text of the Canons is enough to show the ample scriptural testimony that undergirds its teaching. The united testimony of Scripture is that the believer is who he is merely of grace. Were it not for God's electing favor in Christ, the believer would still be in his sins.

The Debate Concerning "Reprobation"

In the recent history of the Reformed churches, a considerable debate has been carried on in the Netherlands and in North America regarding the doctrine of double predestination, particularly the decree of reprobation. A number of voices have been raised against the alleged "scholasticism" of the Canons of Dort, and against what is often disparagingly termed the "decretal theology" of this confession. Often it is argued that we should speak of God's eternal purpose of election, His good pleasure to save His people in Christ, but we should not speak of God's eternal purpose to *pass others by*, "leaving" them in their sin and misery, not granting to them faith and conversion and finally condemning them to suffer eternal punishment for their unbelief and other sins (Article 15). Those who advocate this approach want to insist that the electing purpose of God is solely and singularly gracious. We should avoid, therefore, speaking of God's purpose not to save or to reprobate those whom he passes by in His eternal counsel.[4]

Though the arguments of those who oppose the doctrine of double predestination, particularly the doctrine of reprobation, are diverse, three arguments stand out. The first argument claims that the Scriptures nowhere teach reprobation, but that it is simply a logical conclusion from

---

4. Readers acquainted with the history of the Christian Reformed Church will recognize in this description the position of Harry Boer. Boer has set forth his "case" against the doctrine of reprobation in his book, *The Doctrine of Reprobation in the Christian Reformed Church* (Grand Rapids: Eerdmans, 1983). According to Boer, there is no scriptural support for the doctrine of reprobation. Furthermore, he argues that reprobation makes God the "author" of the unbelief of those who are not elect. Not only is this charge a "false accusation," little more than the old Arminian objection in new dress, but it ignores the Canons' repeated insistence that God elected to save His people "out of the entire human race, which had fallen by its own fault from its original innocence into sin and ruin" (Article 7). It further neglects to note the way the Canons distinguish God's sovereign decision to "leave" some in their sins and their final condemnation "not only for their unbelief but also for all their other sins" (Article 15).

the doctrine of election. The second argument insists that the doctrine of reprobation makes God the author of sin, since it ascribes the fact that some do not believe and repent at the preaching of the gospel to God's counsel. The third argument claims that Scripture only knows a divine election of the church as a corporate body, not an election, to use the language of the Canons, of a "definite number of particular people." According to this argument, we should speak only of the historical-redemptive election of a people, and not of God's eternal decree(s).

How Should We Reply to These Objections?

With respect to the first argument, it should be noted that the scriptural argument for a doctrine of particular election holds equally well for a doctrine of particular non-election or reprobation. The authors of the Canons correctly noted, for this reason, that the Scripture "bears witness that not all people have been chosen but that some have not been chosen or have been passed by in God's eternal election" (Article 15). Unless words no longer have an identifiable meaning, any scriptural passage that teaches God's election of a particular people to salvation, teaches equally God's non-election of others. To say that God "elects" to save some is only to say that some are non-elect. This is not simply a logical inference from the scriptural teaching of particular election. The scriptural teaching that not all are elect means that some are non-elect.

With respect to the second argument, those who claim that reprobation makes God the author of sin ignore not only the express rejections of this as "blasphemy" by the authors of the Canons, but they also ignore the all-important fact that God's counsel of election and reprobation discriminates between people, all of whom are contemplated as fallen in Adam and under the just condemnation of God. To put the matter differently, the fact that some people are not saved does indeed derive from the good pleasure of the triune God. But this does not make God the author of their sin and unbelief. Neither does it make His final condemnation and eternal punishment of the unbelieving and impenitent any less just. For it must be remembered that all sinners fall short of God's glory and are deserving of His condemnation. And though God's good pleasure to save the elect or to pass by the reprobate may be inscrutable to us, it is nonetheless the confident confession of the believer that God does only what is in accord with the highest wisdom and justice.[5]

With respect to the third argument, it is true that we must avoid an individualistic and ahistorical doctrine of election. Scripturally considered, those whom God elects to save comprise the whole body of the church, the chosen bride of Christ. The elect are nothing less than the organic unity of the new humanity in Christ, whom God is pleased to call out of the world of fallen humanity by His Spirit and Word in the unity of the true faith. We should not, therefore, think of the elect as a composite or collective of isolated individuals, like so many "brands plucked from the burning."

However, this corporate and organic unity of the new, elect humanity whom God has chosen to save in Christ is also comprised of individuals whom God gives to Christ. There is an inescapably particular and personal dimension to the scriptural understanding of election. Indeed, to deny that God's election of His people amounts to the election of a definite number of particular persons robs us of the comfort of this teaching. For the comfort of election is identical with the comfort of the gospel, namely, "that *I* . . . am not *my* own, but belong unto *my* faithful Savior Jesus Christ; who with His precious blood has

---

5. In an important conclusion to the Canons, entitled "Rejection of False Accusations," the authors of the Canons explicitly reject the charge that their "teaching means that God predestined and created, by the bare and unqualified choice of his will, without the least regard or consideration of any sin, the greatest part of the world to eternal condemnation." Those today who make this "false accusation" are simply mimicking the Arminians of a previous period. Apparently, they have elected (arbitrarily!) to ignore the clear teaching of the Canons that God's decision not to save the non-elect left them in a circumstance into which they have willfully plunged themselves, and for which God is not to be blamed, as though He were the author of their sin.

fully satisfied for all *my* sins" (Heidelberg Catechism, Q. & A. 1, emphasis mine).

The Preaching of Election

Before concluding this summary of the Canons' teaching on election, something needs to be said yet on the preaching of election. Frequently, it is alleged that it is not possible to preach what the Canons set forth as the scriptural teaching of unconditional election. Because (so it is argued) this confession cannot be preached, it is not biblical.

It is noteworthy that the authors of the Canons were aware of the need to preach election in a wise manner. In Article 14 of the first main point of doctrine, we read:

> Just as, by God's wise plan, this teaching concerning divine election has been proclaimed through the prophets, Christ himself, and the apostles, in Old and New Testament times, and has subsequently been committed to writing in the Holy Scriptures, so also today in God's church, for which it was specifically intended, this teaching must be set forth—with a spirit of discretion, in a godly and holy manner, at the appropriate time and place, without inquisitive searching into the ways of the Most High. This must be done for the glory of God's most holy name, and for the lively comfort of his people.

Reflection on this important affirmation of the confession suggests the following guidelines for the preaching of election.

First: In any ministry or preaching of the Word, the "whole counsel of God," including the teaching of unconditional election, must be preached. God has been pleased, for the edification and salvation of His people, to reveal the truth concerning His electing grace in Christ in the Scriptures. It would be unfaithfulness and ingratitude on our part, not to preach what the Word teaches on this subject.

Second: The preaching of election must be carefully disciplined by the Word of God, declaring neither more nor less than God has been pleased to reveal to us in the Word. This means that we are not to pry "inquisitively" into the subject of election beyond the limits of scriptural revelation.

Third: Though the doctrine of election is at the heart of the gospel, the good news of God's gracious determination to save His people in Christ, it is not the whole of the gospel. All gospel preaching must clearly distinguish between God's eternal purpose to save His people and the concrete way, in the history of redemption, whereby He is pleased to accomplish this purpose. To use the traditional language, the preaching of election must not confuse the purpose of election with the covenantal means God uses to effect this purpose. Since God is pleased to draw His people to Himself through the preaching of the gospel, the preaching of election may not displace or weaken the earnest call to the sinner to respond in faith and repentance.

Fourth: Any preaching of the gospel of God's electing love and purpose in Christ that treats this gospel as a puzzle, separating between God's eternal purpose and the revelation of His grace and kindness in the gospel of Christ, must be rejected. The preaching of election may never be divorced from the call to faith and repentance through the gospel. Nor may it be divorced from the summons that goes out through the gospel to all men without distinction, calling them to faith. Believers must be assured that "their election and calling" are confirmed and established *in Christ*, whom Calvin aptly termed the "mirror" in whom we may contemplate our election.

Fifth: Though it is sometimes argued that reprobation, God's free decision to leave some men in their sin and misery, cannot be preached, this is based on the false assumption that the preaching of reprobation requires that the minister declare some of the congregation to be reprobate. But this is not true. It is every minister's duty to call all to whom the gospel is preached to faith and repentance, *confident* that the Lord will use this means to draw all whom He has chosen to Himself.[6] This same message is preached to all men without discrimination. To employ the language of the Canons, the gospel must be "announced and declared without differentiation [lit. "promiscuously"] or discrimination to all nations and people."

Sixth: The twofold purpose of all preaching of election is God's glory and our comfort. This is the truest test of a biblical pattern of preaching the doctrine of election. Does this preaching glorify God? Does it comfort the believing sinner? It is not the calling of the preacher or the congregation to inquire speculatively into the questions, "Who is elect?" and, "Who is reprobate?" Certainly not! Rather, it is the calling of the preacher to exalt and magnify God's invincible grace in His unmerited favor toward His people in Christ Jesus. Such preaching glorifies God and brings solid comfort.

The Canons themselves conclude with a beautiful petition, appropriate to this subject and fitting as well to close our consideration of their teaching on election:

> May God's Son Jesus Christ, who sits at the right hand of God and gives gifts to men, sanctify us in the truth, lead to the truth those who err, silence the mouths of those who lay false accusations against sound teaching, and equip faithful ministers of his Word with a spirit of wisdom and discretion, that all they say may be to the glory of God and the building up of their hearers. Amen.

---

6. This is a point that J. I. Packer emphasizes in his book, *Evangelism and the Sovereignty of God* (Downers Grove, IL: Intervarsity, 1961). The doctrine of election does not detract from the task of evangelism; it provides the work of evangelism with its dynamic (power) and assures its effectiveness.

Questions for Discussion

1. What was the Arminian position on election? Do you think the Arminian view is prevalent in many churches today? Explain. What is the position of the Canons of Dort on election?

2. Should we begin the proclamation of the gospel with the call to faith and repentance? Why or why not?

3. How would you respond to someone who argued that, "if the number of the elect is fixed, there is no reason to preach the gospel to everyone"?

4. What is meant by "reprobation"? How does election imply reprobation? Show how the Bible teaches reprobation.

5. What's wrong with the statement, "If I'm elect, I'll be saved, no matter what I do"?

6. How does the teaching of election glorify God and comfort believers?

7. Do the Canons of Dort (I, 17) assume too much about the salvation of the children of believers?

Chapter Three

Particular Redemption

The Second Main Point of Doctrine

In the two previous chapters, I introduced the Canons of Dort and considered the "first main point of doctrine," unconditional election. In this chapter we turn to the second, and perhaps most controversial of the "five points," the doctrine of "limited atonement," as it is most commonly known, or of "particular redemption," as I prefer to term it.[1]

Without any doubt this is the most disputed aspect of the summary of scriptural teaching found in the Canons of Dort. It may have been the experience of some readers, as it has been mine, that you have encountered people who term themselves "four-point" Calvinists. These are people who are ready to confess unconditional election, total depravity, irresistible grace and the perseverance of the saints. But they cannot abide the teaching that Christ's atoning work was designed and accomplished only for the elect. Typically, those who resist this component of scriptural teaching argue that it is not consistent with the biblical teaching that "God so loved the *world* that He gave His only-begotten Son . . . ." How—such objectors will frequently protest—can you preach the gospel to all people

---

1. A number of Reformed writers, including J. I. Packer, have argued for the terminology of "particular redemption." I prefer this language myself, for reasons that will be discussed later, but we cannot escape the language of "limited atonement," if for no other reason than the popularity of the acronym "TULIP." As Roger Nicole has remarked, the Dutch love for tulips is such that we cannot easily dispense with this useful acronym.

without discrimination, declaring that "God loves them and Christ died for them," when in fact God only loves the elect and gave Christ as an atoning sacrifice for them, but not for others?

Before prematurely responding to these objections, we need to begin with a summary of the teaching of the Canons on this point. Then, following the precedent of the previous chapter, we need to raise the all-important question—is this the Bible's teaching? After having addressed these two matters, I will return to the two most common objections to this teaching.

The Position of the Canons

Of the five points of doctrine summarized in the Canons, the second is given the briefest treatment. Following the usual order, the framers of the confession begin with a positive statement of the scriptural teaching and conclude with a refutation of errors.

In the first article the Canons begin with the basic scriptural teaching that God, who is not only "supremely merciful" but also "supremely just," demands that "the sins we have committed against his infinite majesty be punished with both temporal and eternal punishments, of soul as well as body." God, to be true to Himself, cannot abide sinful man's rebellion and defection from His just rule. There is no escape for the sinful creature from the consequence of this divine justice.

Within the setting of this fundamental and inescapable reality, the Canons affirm that the only possible way of escape for any sinful creature rests in the gracious provision through God's mercy of a Savior who has satisfied God's justice.

> Since, however, we ourselves cannot give this satisfaction or deliver ourselves from God's anger, God in his boundless mercy has given us as a guarantee his only begotten Son, who was made to be sin and a curse for us, in our place, on the cross, in order that he might give satisfaction for us (Article 2).

No one can be saved, unless Christ's satisfaction of God's justice through His work of atonement is credited to him.

Immediately after establishing the need for Christ's atoning work on the cross, the Canons assert the infinite value and worth of Christ's satisfaction. There is nothing lacking in Christ's satisfaction. Indeed, it "is the only and entirely complete sacrifice and satisfaction for sins" and "is of infinite value and worth, more than sufficient to atone for the sins of the whole world." The church, therefore, has the mandate to proclaim the gospel of salvation through Christ to "all nations and peoples, to whom God in his good pleasure sends the gospel." In her discharge of this mandate, the church is called to proclaim indiscriminately that all who believe in Christ crucified and turn from their sins shall not perish but have eternal life. Consequently, those who do not repent and respond to this gospel call are themselves at fault, and they cannot charge the sacrifice of Christ offered on the cross with any deficiency or insufficiency.

Having established the need for Christ's atoning work, and having affirmed its infinite value and sufficiency, on the basis of which the gospel call is extended to all to repent and believe, the authors of the Canons set forth the central thesis of this second point of doctrine: God designed and Christ effected His atoning work for the elect in particular.

> For it was the entirely free plan and very gracious will and intention of God the Father that the enlivening and saving effectiveness of his Son's costly death should work itself out in all his chosen ones, in order that he might grant justifying faith to them only and thereby lead them without fail to salvation. In other words, it was God's will that Christ through the blood of the cross (by which he confirmed the new covenant) should effectively redeem from every people, tribe, nation, and language all those and only those who were chosen from eternity to salvation and given to him by the Father; that he should grant them faith (which, like the Holy Spirit's other saving gifts, he acquired for them by his death); that he should cleanse them by his

blood from all their sins, both original and actual . . . (Article 8).

There is a perfect harmony in God's counsel and redemptive work between His sovereign good pleasure to save His people and His gracious provision through Christ of the satisfaction required to redeem them. The Father wills to give to the Son those whom He purposed to save and whom the Son redeemed with His precious blood.

The Scriptural Support for This Position

In the text of the Canons, a number of biblical texts are cited in support of the doctrine of limited atonement or particular redemption. Though by no means intended to exhaust the biblical material underlying the Canons' affirmations, these texts reflect three prominent lines of biblical evidence for the teaching of particular redemption.

The Nature of Christ's Saving Work

The first line of biblical evidence is found in those biblical passages that describe Christ's atoning work as actually effecting and not simply making possible the salvation of His people. The biblical terms describing Christ's atoning work can only be understood when they are taken to describe what Christ has done on behalf of His people, not what He would like to accomplish or make available to them.

Accordingly, when the Scriptures describe what Christ has accomplished on behalf of His people, they use expressions that enumerate blessings secured, not blessings yet to be obtained or hanging in the balance. We do not read that Christ made reconciliation obtainable; we read that Christ, by His redeeming work, secured reconciliation (compare Rom. 5:10; 2 Cor. 5:18, 19; Eph. 2:15, 16; Col. 1:15, 16). We do not read that Christ made redemption possible; we read that He redeemed and purchased His people for Himself (compare Rom. 3:24, 25; 1 Cor. 1:30; Gal. 3:13). For example, in Col. 1:13, 14, we read that, "For He delivered us from the domain of darkness, and transferred us to the kingdom of His beloved Son, in whom we have redemption, the forgiveness of sins." Or again in Hebrews 9:12, Christ's sacrifice is described as one by which "He entered the holy place once for all, having obtained eternal redemption." Nor do we read that Christ came to initiate the salvation of His people; we read that He came to save them (compare Matt. 1:21; Luke 19:10; Gal. 1:3, 4; 1 Tim. 1:15).

If the terms employed in the Scriptures to describe the character of Christ's atoning work on our behalf—propitiation, reconciliation, redemption, salvation, and the like—only describe what He has made possible for all, then they lose their meaning. For example, if Christ propitiated the wrath of God against the sins of all men, then surely this means they are no longer under God's wrath and condemnation. Either Christ propitiated God's wrath for them or He did not; and, if He did, they have been delivered from any prospect of a wrath to come. The very nature of Christ's saving work requires that it either secure the salvation of those for whom it was done or be deprived of any saving effectiveness.

The Harmony between Father and Son

Another line of biblical evidence, supporting the teaching of particular redemption, is found in those biblical passages that reveal a harmony of purpose and work between the Father and the Son.[2] To put it more concretely, there is no evidence of a working at cross-purposes between the Father, who purposed from before the foundation of the world to save His people, and the Son, whom the Father sent to redeem the elect and to whom He is pleased to give them as His rightful inheritance (compare Psalm 2).

In the Gospel of John, Christ clearly reveals that He was sent by the Father into the world to save the people whom the Father

---

2. The same unity of purpose and work obtains for the application of Christ's atoning work by the Holy Spirit through the gospel. Since this is a subject more appropriate to the "fourth main point of doctrine," irresistible grace, I will defer consideration of it to a subsequent chapter.

would give to Him. Furthermore, those whom the Father gives Him will not fail to come to Him, and none of them shall be lost. An emphatic declaration of this harmony of purpose and work between the Father and the Son is provided us in John 6:35–40:

> Jesus said to them, "I am the bread of life; he who comes to Me shall not hunger, and he who believes in Me shall never thirst. But I said to you, that you have seen Me, and yet do not believe. All that the Father gives Me shall come to Me, and the one who comes to Me I will certainly not cast out. For I have come down from heaven, not to do My own will, but the will of Him who sent me. And this is the will of Him who sent Me, that of all that He has given Me I lose nothing, but raise it up on the last day."

In a similar vein, when describing Himself as the good shepherd who lays down His life for His sheep, Christ teaches that these sheep, whom He knows and who know Him, are precisely those whom the Father wills to give to Him.

> I am the good shepherd; the good shepherd lays down His life for the sheep. . . . I am the good shepherd; and I know My own, and My own know Me, even as the Father knows Me and I know the Father; and I lay down My life for the sheep. And I have other sheep, which are not of this fold; I must bring them also, and they shall hear My voice; and they shall become one flock with one shepherd. For this reason the Father loves Me, because I lay down My life that I may take it again. No one has taken it away from Me, but I lay it down on My own initiative. I have authority to lay it down, and I have authority to take it up again. This commandment I received from My Father. (John 10:11, 14–18)

In these and other passages (compare John 10:24–29; John 17:1–11,20, 24–26; Eph. 1:3–12; Rom. 5:12, 17–19), the priestly work of Christ in the redemption of His people accomplishes the purpose for which the Father sent and gave Him. There is not a hint of uncertainty about the objects (who are His sheep) or the perfection (will the good shepherd be able to save His flock) of Christ's saving work. The Father's will and purpose is invincible—He will give them to the Son. The Son's purchase of their redemption is certain—He has power to lay down His life and take it up again. There is a "regal" quality to the gospel descriptions of Christ's atoning purpose and work; like a conquering king He offers Himself a sacrifice to secure without fail the salvation of His people.[3]

The Particular Objects of Christ's Redemption

A third and final line of biblical evidence supporting the teaching of particular redemption is found in those passages that speak of Christ's atoning work on behalf of a particular or definite people. The Scriptures do not present Christ's work as being done on behalf of an indiscriminate and indefinite people; they present His work as directed to the redemption of the elect, the "beloved" of God.

Before noting some of these passages, it should be acknowledged that there are also passages in Scripture that speak of Christ's saving work in very broad and general terms. Some of these passages speak of His work on behalf of the "world" (e.g.: John 1:9, 29; 3:16, 17; 4:42; 2 Cor. 5:19;

---

3. This is a good place to note the position of Moise Amyraut, a French Reformed theologian of the seventeenth century, who attempted to find a mediating position on the atonement between Reformed and Arminian views. Known as "Amyraldianism" or the doctrine of "hypothetical universalism," this position distinguished a twofold decree of God: one, to send Christ into the world to save *all* men by His atoning death on the condition of faith; and two, to give to the elect a special grace enabling them to believe and secure their redemption through Christ. This view seeks to combine an "unlimited atonement" with a doctrine of "particular redemption." The discerning reader will notice, of course, that it does so at the price of sacrificing the effectiveness of Christ's atoning work on behalf of all for whom He made atonement. It also posits a conflict between the Son's *universal work* of atonement and the Father's *particular purpose* of election.

1 John 2:1, 2; 4:14); others speak of His work on behalf of "all" men (e.g.: Rom. 5:18; 2 Cor. 5:14, 15; 1 Tim. 2:4–6; Heb. 2:9; 2 Pet. 3:9). Often critics of the doctrine of limited atonement will cite these passages as clearly refuting the idea that Christ's redemptive work was directed to the salvation of a particular people, the elect.

These are indeed important passages that must not be overlooked or discounted in any consideration of the extent of Christ's work of atonement. They clearly underscore the broad and universal scope of Christ's work of redemption. They also remind us that God wants the gospel preached to everyone, not willing that any should perish (1 Tim. 2:4; 2 Pet. 3:9). They remind us that God wants the gospel preached as an earnest summons to everyone to turn in faith and salvation, finding salvation in Jesus Christ.

However, it should be noted that these passages must be read in their immediate, scriptural context. They must be understood according to the rule, "Scripture interprets Scripture." When these passages are interpreted in their context and according to this rule, it becomes evident that they only teach that Christ died for all men *without distinction* (that is, for Jews as well as Gentiles, for slave as well as free). Christ's atoning work effects the salvation of a new humanity, a people comprised of sinners from every tribe, people, nation and language. But these passages do not teach that Christ died for all men *without exception* (that is, for the purpose of saving each and every sinner).[4]

In the context of the teaching of the whole of Scripture (*totus Scripturae*), there are a great number of passages that clearly delimit the design and effect of Christ's atoning work to a particular people whose salvation He secures. Consider the following passages as a sampling: Matt. 1:21, "for it is He who will save His people from their sins"; John 10:11, "I am the

---

4. Cf. David N. Steele & Curtis C. Thomas, eds., *The Five Points of Calvinism: Defined, Defended, Documented* (New Jersey: Presbyterian & Reformed Publishing Co., 1963), p. 46, whose distinction I am using here.

good shepherd. The good shepherd lays down his life for the sheep"; John 11:51–52, "he [Caiaphas] prophesied that Jesus was going to die for the nation, and not for the nation only, but that He might also gather together into one the children of God who are scattered abroad"; Acts 20:28, "Be on guard for yourselves and for all the flock, among which the Holy Spirit has made you overseers, to shepherd the church of God which He purchased with his own blood"; Eph. 5:25, "Husbands, love your wives, just as Christ also loved the church and gave Himself up for her"; Rom. 8:32–33, "He who did not spare His own Son, but delivered Him up for us all, how will He not also with Him freely give us all things? Who will bring a charge against God's elect?"; Heb. 9:15, "He is the mediator of a new covenant, in order that . . . those who have been called may receive the promise of the eternal inheritance"; and Rev. 5:9, "And they sang a new song, saying, 'Worthy art Thou to take the book, and to break its seals; for Thou wast slain, and didst purchase for God with Thy blood men from every tribe and tongue and people and nation.'"

In this connection, it is also instructive to observe how the language of Scripture restricts God's redemptive love in Christ to His chosen people. Consistent with those passages that speak of Christ dying for a particular people whose salvation He secures with His own precious blood, this language is particular and definite. To cite but two examples, notice the way the saints are addressed in 1 Thessalonians 1:2, 4 ("We give thanks to God always for all of you, making mention of you in our prayers . . . knowing, brethren *beloved by God*, His choice of you") or in Colossians 3:12 ("as those who have been chosen of God, holy and *beloved*"). These kinds of expressions appear almost incidental to us, but they reflect a profound awareness of the particularity and definiteness of God's love in Christ for His own. Just as a husband sets His affection and love on His own wife, and on no other, so the Lord, being a perfectly faithful bridegroom, sets His affection and love on the church, His bride.

Two Common Objections

Earlier I referred to the fact that this point of doctrine, particular redemption, is the most disputed and often refuted of the five points of doctrine summarized in the Canons of Dort. Though we cannot enter into the full debate over this subject, there are two common objections to this teaching that we need to consider.

Christ's Atonement Is Limited

The first of these objections is that the doctrine of particular redemption improperly limits Christ's atoning work. If Christ's redemptive work is limited in its extent to the elect, those whom the Father purposes to save and gives to the Son, then its value is diminished. Such a limitation on the extent of Christ's atoning work belittles what He has accomplished for all men.

At first glance this objection seems to have some punch. However, on closer examination it loses its persuasiveness.

In the first place, the Canons emphatically affirm the value and sufficiency of Christ's atoning work to save every sinner without exception. The authors of the Canons begin their treatment of this point of doctrine by underscoring just this truth—there is nothing lacking in Christ's atoning work.

Moreover, some limitation on Christ's work of atonement is unavoidable, unless we become "universalists" and teach the salvation of all. The Remonstrant or Arminian position limits Christ's work of atonement in respect to its effectiveness and security. According to the Remonstrant position, Christ's saving work was designed to make salvation possible for all men, provided that they respond in faith and repentance. In itself the atoning work of Christ did not and does not secure or guarantee the salvation of any one in particular. Furthermore, since the Remonstrants admitted that not all are finally saved, they also were compelled to acknowledge that, however possible the salvation of all may be on the basis of Christ's atoning work, Christ's work was actually only an atonement for those who believe.

The Canons, summarizing the teaching of Scripture, affirm by contrast that the atoning work of Christ is fully and completely effective on behalf of all those for whom it was accomplished. Though this might be termed a "limitation" on the extent of the atonement, this is not so much a doctrine of limited atonement as it is a doctrine of *definite* atonement. For this reason, I prefer the language of "particular redemption," for it removes any suggestion of deficiency with respect to Christ's saving work. The Reformed, biblical position teaches that Christ's atoning work fully secures that for which it was designed. Or, to employ an analogy offered by Boettner, for the Canons the atonement of Christ "is like a narrow bridge which goes all the way across the stream; for the Arminian it is like a great wide bridge that goes only half-way across."[5]

The Indiscriminate Preaching of the Gospel Is Undermined

Another objection, perhaps even more common than this first one, to the doctrine of limited atonement, alleges that it undermines any motive for the indiscriminate preaching of the gospel. How, those who raise this objection ask, can the gospel be preached to everyone without distinction, "promiscuously," to use the language of the Canons, when Christ died only for the elect? How can the minister of the Word declare the good news of Christ's death on behalf of sinners, when many to whom the gospel is preached were not included in the design, nor will they benefit from Christ's work of atonement?

Though this particular objection played a major role in the "love of God controversy" in the Christian Reformed Church

---

5. Loraine Boettner, *The Reformed Doctrine of Predestination* (Philadelphia: Presbyterian & Reformed Publishing Co., 1963), p. 153.

during the 1960s,[6] I fail to see its force. Those who object to the teaching of particular redemption argue that this hinders an aggressive presentation of the gospel and prevents the minister from declaring to any and all, "God loves you, and Christ died for you."

On both counts this objection fails. In the first place, the greatest possible encouragement to an unhindered proclamation of the gospel derives from the confidence that by this means Christ will unfailingly communicate the benefits of His atoning work to all those whose salvation that work secured. What a great encouragement to the missionary calling of the church— to be privileged to declare the unsearchable riches of God's grace in Christ, who has ransomed for Himself through His atoning sacrifice a vast multitude whom no man can number from every tribe, tongue, people and nation. The preaching of this gospel does not have to labor under the impossible burden of persuading people to do for themselves what Christ has left undone. Rather, it can call all without distinction to believe in Him as a complete and perfect Savior of His people.

In the second place, there is no authorization, either by way of direct command or apostolic example, for any preaching of the gospel that indiscriminately declares to everyone, "God loves you, and Christ died for you." Such a declaration is palpably false, even on an Arminian basis (for Christ finally dies only for those who benefit from His death). The gospel proclaims the death of Christ to all sinners, promising the benefits of this

---

6. The controversy focused on the writings of Harold Dekker, professor of missions at Calvin Seminary, who attempted to modify the classical language and understanding of "limited atonement" by speaking of a universal "redemptive love" of God toward all men. Dekker argued that the traditional confession of "limited atonement" was a hindrance to the missionary task of the church and prevented the minister from proclaiming the message of God's love and Christ's death on behalf of sinners to all without discrimination. The controversy, though formally resolved by the Christian Reformed Synod of 1967, did not come to a satisfactory or clear conclusion. The recent writings of Rev. Neal Punt in defense of "biblical universalism" represent a new chapter in this unfinished history.

death only to those who believe and repent. Hence, the gospel is to be preached, not as a comfort blanket thrown over all, assuring them of Christ's death on their behalf, but as an urgent appeal, commanding all to repent (Acts 17) and to turn to Christ in faith. Only within the framework of such a repenting and believing is the minister of the gospel authorized to declare with confidence the love of God and the riches of His mercy toward us in Christ.

Admittedly, Reformed preachers have sometimes drawn the wrong conclusion from this and been too hesitant and reserved to preach the gospel indiscriminately, to everyone. This needs to be acknowledged and corrected. The preacher of the gospel is authorized, even mandated, to declare God's earnest and sincere call in the gospel, inviting faith and repentance from all. Though this may appear to conflict with the gospel of unconditional election and particular redemption, it is the clear message of the Scriptures. God takes no pleasure in the death of anyone, but calls all to embrace Christ in faith. Nevertheless, when he proclaims the gospel of Christ, the preacher is not permitted to say that God loves and provides atonement in Christ for everyone.

Conclusion

When a Reformed believer reflects on the scriptural teaching of particular redemption, he realizes quickly that nothing less than the glorious perfection and effectiveness of Christ's saving work is at issue. However controversial and disputed may be this point of the Canons' summary of scriptural teaching, then, the Reformed believer must cling tenaciously to this point as well as the others.[7]

Why? Because the gospel message is good news, not of a Savior who does what He can for us, but of a Savior who saves to the uttermost. Because the gospel message is focused on a perfect Savior, the good shepherd who knows His sheep and whose sheep hear His voice. These sheep belong to that precious flock whom the Father has promised to give to the Son and whom no one can snatch from His hand. This is a gospel whose Savior is worthy of praise unending and whose comfort is sure. Indeed, it is the only gospel that may be preached with confidence to the nations.

Recommended Reading:

Berkhof, Louis. *Vicarious Atonement through Christ.* Grand Rapids: Eerdmans, 1936.

Kuiper, R. B. *For Whom Did Christ Die?* Grand Rapids: Eerdmans, 1959.

Murray, John. *Redemption: Accomplished and Applied.* Grand Rapids: Eerdmans, 1955.

---

7. Though I have not stressed it in this chapter, it is simply impossible to reject the doctrine of "particular redemption" without undermining all the five main points of doctrine affirmed by the Canons. Not only does a doctrine of "universal" or "indefinite" atonement conflict with the Scripture's teaching concerning sovereign election, but it is also inconsistent with the Scripture's teaching of total depravity, irresistible grace, and the perseverance of the saints. The phrase, "four-point Calvinist," is an oxymoron, a contradiction in terms.

Questions for Discussion

1. What was the position of the Arminians on the extent of Christ's work of atonement? Do you believe that this is commonly the position of Christians today? Explain.

2. What is the position of the Canons of Dort on the extent of Christ's work of atonement?

3. Would it be better to use language other than "limited atonement"? Why or why not? Would you agree with the preacher Spurgeon's contention that Arminians "limit" the atoning work of Christ? How would you defend your answer?

4. What is the connection between unconditional election and particular atonement?

5. In what sense did Jesus "bear the wrath of God against the sin of the whole human race" (Heidelberg Catechism, Lord's Day 15)?

6. Why should the gospel be preached to all persons "promiscuously and without distinction"?

Chapter Four

Total Depravity

The Third Main Point of Doctrine

When we think of the Canons of Dort and their five main points of doctrine, we usually organize our thoughts according to the sequence of letters in the acronym "TULIP." We begin, accordingly, with the letter "T," which stands for "total depravity."

Though this is not the order in which the authors of the Canons of Dort presented their confession of the biblical teaching concerning salvation by grace alone—as we have seen in previous chapters, the five main points of doctrine followed the order of the five points of the Remonstrance or Arminian position—there is an important sense in which this point is first. The biblical teaching concerning man's condition as a sinner, unable and incompetent to save himself, is the setting within which the biblical teaching of salvation by God's grace alone flourishes. This point of doctrine illustrates what we have already emphasized in our previous chapters: the close connection and interrelationship of each of the five points set forth in the Canons. Only God's unconditional election and saving work in Christ on behalf of His people answer to the needs of a totally depraved sinner. But for the grace of God toward us in Christ, our situation would be utterly hopeless.

It is to this that the third main point of doctrine, total depravity, speaks. Here the Canons of Dort set forth a biblical view of man in his sin before the face of God.

And they do so in service of the one, great theme—God's grace alone answers to our plight.

The Position of the Canons

When you read the Canons of Dort, you will immediately notice that the third and fourth main points of doctrine are treated together (the fourth main point is the doctrine of "irresistible grace").

This is so for an obvious reason. How you understand man's condition has everything to do with the way you understand God's saving work. If sinful man is simply wounded or sick spiritually, but not wholly dead, he will not require the kind of redemption geared to the circumstance of one altogether dead. It does not take the same kind of work to resuscitate someone whose pulse is weak and whose breath is short, as it does to grant new life to a dead corpse. Because of the close relationship, then, between these two points of doctrine, the one dealing with man's sinful condition and the other with the Spirit's saving work, we will not be able to avoid touching on the fourth main point of doctrine as we proceed.[1]

The position of the Canons on the plight of sinful man is starkly portrayed in the first five articles of this section of the confession.

---

1. It should be noted that, in the history of controversy in the Netherlands between the Remonstrants (Arminians) and the contra-Remonstrants, there was an apparent agreement on this third main point of doctrine. The contra-Remonstrants did not object to the third article of the Remonstrance of 1610, dealing with the subject of the extent of sinful man's depravity and need for the regenerating grace of God. This accounts in part for the treatment of the third and fourth main points of doctrine together in the Counter Remonstrance of 1611 and the Canons of Dort. Of course, as we shall see, this agreement on the third main point of doctrine was only formal and apparent. The difference between the Remonstrants and the contra-Remonstrants on the fourth main point of doctrine, irresistible grace, shows that they were not truly agreed on the extent of sinful man's depravity.

In the first article, a sharp contrast is drawn between man's original state of integrity, as he was created by God, and his sinful state after the fall.

> Man was originally created in the image of God and was furnished in his mind with a true and salutary knowledge of his Creator and things spiritual, in his will and heart with righteousness, and in all his emotions with purity; indeed, the whole man was holy. However, rebelling against God at the devil's instigation and by his own free will, he deprived himself of these outstanding gifts. Rather, in their place he brought upon himself blindness, terrible darkness, futility, and distortion of judgment in his mind; perversity, defiance, and hardness in his heart and will; and finally impurity in all his emotions (Article 1).

Any consideration of the human predicament before God must be founded on a clear understanding of this contrast. Though man was originally created good and perfect, bearing God's image and able to live in unbroken communion with his Creator, he has become through the fall into sin a rebel against God, unable and unwilling to live in that communion with his Creator for which he was first created.

In Articles 2 and 3 of this section of the Canons of Dort, the spread of this corruption of sin to the whole human race (Article 2) and the consequent total inability of the sinner to save himself (Article 3) are affirmed. All of the children of Adam bear a family likeness, in the sense that "man brought forth children of the same nature as himself after the fall." With the single exception of Christ, who was born "of Adam" (Luke 3:38), yet without sin, all members of the fallen human race share in a common corruption or hereditary depravity. This corruption is not to be understood as having been spread by imitation, as the Pelagians teach, but by "the propagation of his perverted nature." This corruption renders sinful man incapable of saving himself. Because of the importance of this consequence of man's sinful condition, the language of the Canons requires careful consideration:

> Therefore, all people are conceived in sin and are born children of wrath, unfit for any saving good, inclined to evil, dead in their sins, and slaves to sin; without the grace of the regenerating Holy Spirit they are neither willing nor able to return to God, to reform their distorted nature, or even to dispose themselves to such reform[2] (Article 3).

The remainder of the Canons' statement of the depraved condition of sinful man stresses the inadequacy of any means or resource available to him by which he might partially contribute to, assist, or cooperate with God's grace in his own salvation. Neither "the light of nature" (Article 4) nor the law of God (Article 5) is adequate to sinful man's need. With respect to the former, sinful man only distorts the truth and renders himself without excuse before God. With respect to the latter, sinful man only demonstrates the magnitude of his sin and increasingly convicts himself of his guilt before God. The natural man is incompetent to profit from whatever "light of nature" is available to him, or to obtain life through works done in obedience to the law.

In the history of the Reformed churches, there has been a great deal of debate about the Canons' position on total depravity. Most readers of the Canons have rightly observed that their teaching does not claim that sinful man is *absolutely* depraved, in the sense that his sinful nature expresses itself in the fullest and worst possible manner. The point of the Canons is to say that sinful man is *pervasively* depraved; no part of his nature remains uncorrupted or unaffected by sin, so that in all his affections and actions he is a slave to sin.

---

2. The Heidelberg Catechism makes a very similar statement in Lord's Day III, Q. & A. 8: "But are we so corrupt that we are wholly incapable of doing any good, and inclined to all evil? Yes, indeed; unless we are regenerated by the Spirit of God."

In connection with this emphasis on the pervasiveness of man's depravity, the question has also been posed whether sinful man is capable of doing any "good," short of contributing to his own salvation. Appealing to Article 4 of the Canons, most Reformed theologians have maintained that the natural man is able to do some relative good in certain areas. In the language of the Canons, "There is, to be sure, a certain light of nature remaining in man after the fall, by virtue of which he retains some notions about God, natural things, and the difference between what is moral and immoral, and demonstrates a certain eagerness for virtue and for good outward behavior." However, nothing of this enables the sinner to come to a knowledge of God and conversion to Him. Nor does it enable the sinner to do anything "good" in the strict sense, that is, as a fruit of true faith, to the glory of God, and in accordance with the standard of God's law.[3]

Thus, the argument of the Canons is that, though sinful man is not absolutely depraved, and though he may be capable of some limited, relative "good," he is in no condition to do any saving good.

---

3. I am echoing here the language of the Heidelberg Catechism in its definition of "good works." In Lord's Day XXXIII, Q. & A. 91, we read: "But what are good works? Only those which are done from true faith, according to the law of God, and to His glory; and not such as are based on our own opinions or the precepts of men." The question as to whether unregenerate sinners are capable of doing any kind of "good works" has been posed most vigorously in the Reformed churches by Herman Hoeksema and the Protestant Reformed Churches. Not only did Hoeksema argue that the reprobate are incapable of doing any "good" of any kind, but he also rejected the doctrine of "common grace" by which many Reformed theologians have attempted to defend simultaneously the total depravity of the sinner and his capacity (owing to the influence of "common grace") to do some, relative good. At the risk of disturbing the peace of some theologians, I would suggest that the difference between Hoeksema and his opponents on the question of the natural man's ability to do some "good" was to a great extent terminological. Provided there is a willingness to keep the debate over common grace out of the picture, both sides of the debate agree on the key *confessional* point—the sinner is wholly incapable of doing any saving good.

The Scriptural Support for This Position

The confession of man's total depravity or inability to save himself is amply supported in the Scriptures. This is evident from the scriptural descriptions of the sinner's spiritual deadness, blindness and enslavement to the dominion of sin. It is also evident from those scriptural passages that teach that the sinner is lost, apart from the sovereign initiative and working of God by His Spirit in regeneration.

When the condition of the sinner is described in Scripture, this condition is often described as one of spiritual "death." Through the sin of Adam, all men have been born in sin and are by nature in a situation of spiritual death (Gen. 2:16, 17; Rom. 5:12; Ps. 51:5). Only by means of a new beginning, a new creative work of the Holy Spirit, are sinners able to become God's children through adoption and enter the kingdom of heaven (John 3:5–7). One of the most striking affirmations of this is found in Ephesians 2:1–3, where the apostle Paul, describing the circumstance of all believers apart from God's grace in Christ, says: "And you were dead in your trespasses and sins, in which you formerly walked according to the course of this world, according to the prince of the power of the air . . . ." Similarly, in Colossians 2:13 we read, "And when you were dead in your transgressions and the uncircumcision of your flesh, He made you alive together with [Christ]. . . ." Without the life-giving work of God's Spirit, the condition of sinful man, including those who are numbered among the people of God (compare the vision given the prophet Ezekiel of the people of God as a heap of dry bones in Ezekiel 37), is one of death.

Consistent with this condition of spiritual deadness, the Scriptures also describe the sinner as one who is spiritually blind and unable to hear the truth of God's Word. Not only is the heart of the sinner, out of which are the issues of life, corrupt and evil (compare Gen. 6:5; Gen. 8:21; Eccles. 9:3; Jer. 17:9), but also his mind is by nature darkened and incapable of receiving the things of God (John 3:19). In Romans 8:7, 8, the apostle Paul writes that "the mind set on the flesh is hostile to God; for it does not subject itself to the law of God, for it is not even able to do so; and those who are in the flesh cannot please God." In another passage, describing the natural man's blindness to the things of the Spirit, we are taught that "a natural man does not accept the things of the Spirit of God; for they are foolishness to him, and he cannot understand them, because they are spiritually discerned" (1 Cor. 2:14). Apart from the illumination of the Spirit through the Word, sinners can only walk in the "futility of their mind, being darkened in their understanding . . ." (Eph. 4:17–19; compare Eph. 5:8; Tit. 1:15).

Furthermore, the Scriptures often portray the sinner as one who is no longer free to seek God, but a slave to sin. Confronting the unbelief of many who did not receive him in faith, Jesus speaks in the Gospel of John of those who, as children of their father the devil, will to do their father's desire (John 8:44; compare 1 John 3:10). In 2 Timothy 2:25, 26, the predicament of impenitent sinners is compared to those who have been ensnared by the devil and "captured by him to do his will." Frequently, unbelieving sinners are compared to slaves, those who are not masters of their own destiny but witting or unwitting bondservants to sin (compare 1 John 5:19; John 8:34; Tit. 3:3). In an extended comparison in Romans 6, the situation of the unbeliever is contrasted with that of the believer; the unbeliever is one who is a slave to sin and unrighteousness, whereas the believer is one who has been "freed from sin and enslaved to God" (Romans 6:22).[4]

---

4. One of the classic ways of expressing this is to speak of the "bondage of the will" (Luther). The sinner is not free to seek after God unless God gives this freedom. Sometimes this position is caricatured to mean that sinners are somehow prevented from entering the kingdom, even though they desire to enter, or conversely, that God in grace coerces those whom he saves into the kingdom against their will. Nothing could be farther from the truth. We must always remember that the human will is moved by what we find to be desirable. Hence, because the natural man finds God undesirable, he does not will to seek after him; because the regenerate man finds God desirable, he willingly seeks after him. The point is: the natural man has no "will of desire" to receive the things of God or respond to God.

Corresponding to these various metaphors, describing the condition of the sinner as one of spiritual death, blindness, and enslavement, the biblical language employed to describe God's saving work underscores its sovereign graciousness and power. Only God through the Spirit can grant the "new birth" required for the sinner to see and enter the kingdom (John 3:5–7). Only God can take an otherwise dead sinner and make him live again (Romans 8:5–11; Eph. 2:4–7). Only God can do a work such that we become a "new creation" in Christ (2 Cor. 5:17; Eph. 2:10). Only God has the means required to save totally depraved sinners (compare Job 14:4; Jer. 13:23; Matt. 7:16–18; Matt. 12:33; John 6:44). No more than a dead man could walk, no more than a blind man could see, no more than a slave could free himself—no more could a sinner, apart from God's saving recreation of him in Christ by the Spirit, save himself.

Misrepresenting the Position of the Remonstrants?

One objection often registered against the framers of the Canons of Dort is that they misrepresent the position of the Remonstrants or the Arminians on this third main point of doctrine. Did the Remonstrants actually teach that sinful man is able to do some saving good or exercise some power of "free will" to choose to cooperate with the grace of God? Some have cited the statements of the Arminians on this third main point of doctrine in order to maintain that, on this point at least, there was really no difference between the Reformed and the Arminian parties.

Though the Remonstrants or Arminians did present the Synod of Dort with some statements concerning the total depravity of the sinner that appear unobjectionable,[5] their primary emphasis fell on the capacity of the sinner, helped, to be sure, by the general or common grace of God, to resist or not resist the working of the Spirit through the gospel. According to the "Opinions" of the Remonstrants, it is most important to recognize that sinful man must predispose himself to receive and cooperate with the grace of God in order to be saved. Speaking of the former, the sinner's predisposition to receive God's grace, the Remonstrants declared that "to hear the Word of God, to be sorry for sins committed, to desire saving grace and the Spirit of renewal (none of which things man is able to do without grace) are not only not harmful and useless, but rather most useful and most necessary for the *obtaining* of faith and of the Spirit of renewal" (emphasis mine).[6] Though acknowledging the necessity of some working of God's grace to enable this predisposition, the Arminians insisted that this was the sinner's contribution and help, without which the grace of God would be of no effect to save.

Furthermore, the Remonstrants insisted that the grace of God in the gospel is a general or common working of God that enables all who hear the gospel to believe or not believe, repent or not repent. Thus, the salvation of some sinners who believe and repent at the preaching of the gospel is ultimately based on the sinner's willingness or unwillingness to believe.

---

5. See Note 1 above. The Synod of Dort requested and received from the Remonstrant or Arminian party their "Opinions" on the five main points of doctrine (in the Latin: *Sententiae*). The first of these "Opinions" on the third main point of doctrine, when read by itself, has a ring of orthodoxy about it: "Man does not have saving faith of himself, nor out of the powers of his free will, since in the state of sin he is able of himself and by himself neither to think, will, or do any good. . . . It is necessary therefore that by God in Christ through his Holy Spirit he be regenerated and renewed in intellect, affections, will, and in all his powers, so that he might be able to understand, reflect upon, will and carry out the good things which pertain to salvation" (quoted from: Peter Y. De Jong, ed., *Crisis in the Reformed Churches* [Grand Rapids: Reformed Fellowship, Inc., 1968, 2008], p. 244).

6. P. Y. De Jong, ed., *Crisis*, p. 265.

The decisive step in the process of salvation, God having provided a sufficient grace to all men without distinction enabling this step to be taken, lies with the sinner. Whether a sinner is saved or not depends finally on whether he wills to run and to do, not on the sovereign grace, initiative, and provision of salvation by the triune God.

But for the Grace of God

Lest anyone regard the difference between Reformed and Arminian on this point too subtle or inconsequential, it is necessary to remember what I said by way of introduction. Much depends on our diagnosis of man's condition before God. Because the biblical teaching of salvation by grace alone answers to man's need, it can only flourish where this need is clearly and honestly acknowledged. Consequently, in this third main point of doctrine, total depravity, the whole matter of salvation by grace alone once more hangs in the balance.

Rather than make this point in my own words, I would like to conclude with a fitting statement of James I. Packer. In this statement, Packer nicely shows how our understanding of God's saving work and the sinner's miserable condition are intimately joined:

> For to Calvinism there is really only *one* point to be made in the field of soteriology [the doctrine of salvation]: the point that *God saves sinners*. God—the Triune Jehovah, Father, Son and Spirit; three Persons working together in sovereign wisdom, power and love to achieve the salvation of a chosen people, the Father electing, the Son fulfilling the Father's will by redeeming, the Spirit executing the purpose of Father and Son by renewing. *Saves*—does everything, first to last, that is involved in bringing man from death in sin to life in glory; plans, achieves and communicates redemption, calls and keeps, justifies, sanctifies, glorifies. *Sinners*—men as God finds

them, guilty, vile, helpless, powerless, unable to lift a finger to do God's will or better their spiritual lot.[7]

Questions for Discussion

1. Why do the Canons of Dort treat the third and fourth main points of doctrine together (total depravity and irresistible grace)?

2. Summarize the Arminian view of man's sinful condition. Summarize the view of the Canons of Dort.

3. The Canons of Dort do not use the phrase, "total depravity." Can you think of a better phrase to describe man's corrupt or sinful condition? What common terms does the Bible use to describe man's sinful condition?

4. In what sense could you call any of the deeds of unregenerate men "good"? Why would someone object to calling anything the unregenerate do "good"?

5. What is meant by "common grace"? How would you defend the idea of "common grace" from the Bible?

6. What is the weakness of the law of God in the salvation of man, according to Article III–IV, 5 of the Canons of Dort?

7. What is meant by the "freedom of the will"? How is man's possession of a will related to his moral responsibility? Do sinners, apart from the sovereign work of God's grace, have the "free will" to choose for or against God?

---

7. James I. Packer, "Introductory Essay" in John Owen's *The Death of Death in the Death of Christ* (Carlisle, Pennsylvania: Banner of Truth Trust, reprint), p. 6.

Chapter Five

Irresistible Grace

The Fourth Main Point of Doctrine

In the previous chapter, addressing the subject of "total depravity," I concluded with a statement of J. I. Packer in which he argues that the whole point of Calvinism is that *God saves sinners.* The triune God alone authors and accomplishes the salvation of His people; He does not simply make salvation possible, and then leave to the sinner the most decisive step. He actually saves sinners, men and women who lie in the midst of death and who are wholly incapable of doing for themselves what must be done in order that they might be saved.

Nowhere does this fundamental emphasis of Calvinism come to sharper expression than in the fourth main point of doctrine of the Canons of Dort, irresistible grace. The salvation of God's people is the work of the triune God, Father, Son, and Holy Spirit. Founded on the Father's election to save His people for the sake of Christ, His Son, and provided through the atoning work of Christ, the Mediator—salvation is effected and realized by means of the Spirit working irresistibly through the ministry of the gospel.

The doctrine of irresistible grace is addressed, then, to the manner in which the Father's electing purpose and the Son's atoning sacrifice are applied to the hearts and lives of those who are being saved.

The Position of the Canons

The Canons of Dort begin their treatment of the work of
the Spirit in the application of redemption by stressing God's
freedom to reveal His saving will to whom He pleases.
This accounts for the fact that under the old covenant, in
contrast to the new, the saving mercy of God was only disclosed
to a small number of people.

However, in the new covenant the gospel has been
published and must be published to all the nations.
In this publication of the gospel, God "seriously and most
genuinely . . . makes known in his Word what is pleasing
to him: that those who are called should come to him.
Seriously he also promises rest for their souls and eternal life
to all who come to him and believe" (Article 8).[1] This means
that the blame does not belong with Christ or the gospel, when
sinners refuse to believe and repent when called to do so through
the gospel. God sincerely calls everyone through the Word of the
gospel to believe, promising salvation to all without distinction
who answer this call through faith and repentance. The fault
for the unbelief and impenitence of many is, therefore, entirely
their own.

But what about those who do believe and repent, who
are converted, at the preaching of the gospel? Are they to be
credited for their faith and repentance, as though these were
their own accomplishment? The authors of the Canons answer
this question, first, by denying that such faith and repentance
are to be credited to the believer, and second, by affirming that
they are the fruit of the Spirit's working through the gospel.

The fact that others who are called through the ministry
of the gospel do come and are brought to conversion

---

1. It is interesting to note that the language of the Canons, describing the
serious and genuine call that God issues through the gospel to all, is virtually
identical with that employed by the Remonstrants in their fourth article.
However, the Reformed authors of the Canons refused to follow the "logic"
of the Remonstrants or Arminians, who drew the conclusion that all sinners
must then be able of themselves to comply with the gospel's demands.

must not be credited to man, as though one distinguishes himself by free choice from others who are furnished with equal or sufficient grace for faith and conversion (as the proud heresy of Pelagius maintains). No, it must be credited to God: just as from eternity he chose his own in Christ, so within time he effectively calls them, grants them faith and repentance, and, having rescued them from the dominion of darkness, brings them into the kingdom of his Son, in order that they may declare the wonderful deeds of him who called them out of darkness into this marvelous light, and may boast not in themselves, but in the Lord, as apostolic words frequently testify in Scripture (Article 10).

Thus, the Spirit graciously gives to the elect through the call and preaching of the gospel that faith and repentance that are required.

In the following articles of the Canons, the authors attempt, to the extent this is possible, to provide a biblical account of the manner of the Spirit's working in the heart and life of the believer.

Speaking of the Spirit's work in applying the gospel, the Canons affirm that God by the Spirit powerfully enlightens the mind of the believer "so that they may rightly understand and discern the things of the Spirit of God" (Article 11). Furthermore, by "the effective operation of the same regenerating Spirit," God also "penetrates into the inmost being of man, opens the closed heart, softens the hard heart, and circumcises the heart that is uncircumcised." This work of the Spirit includes: giving to the sinner's will, otherwise captivated to sin, the readiness to do good; making the will, otherwise dead and lifeless to the things of God, begin to live and become receptive to the gospel's call; making the will, otherwise unwilling because unable, begin to desire the right; and activating and enlivening the will, otherwise inactive and lifeless, to produce the good fruits that come from a tree that has been made good. In so doing, the Spirit of God effectively enables the sinner, by nature spiritually dead and in bondage to sin, to turn willingly in repentance and faith to God.

The authors of the Canons acknowledge, in their efforts to describe this working of the Spirit, that it is a work altogether marvelous and divine (or supernatural). Accordingly, the things with which it is compared in the Scriptures are the act of (new) creation, the raising of one from the dead, the making alive of what is otherwise lifeless and immobile (Article 12). It is certainly a more powerful and effective working than an act of moral persuasion, which leaves the sinner in the state in which he is found and leaves to the sinner's power the decision to be born again.

> Rather, it is an entirely supernatural work, one that is at the same time most powerful and most pleasing, a marvelous, hidden, and inexpressible work, which is not lesser than or inferior in power to that of creation or of raising the dead. ... As a result, all those in whose hearts God works in this marvelous way are certainly, unfailingly, and effectively reborn and do actually believe. And then the will, now renewed, is not only activated and motivated by God but in being activated by God is also itself active. For this reason, man himself, by that grace which he has received is also rightly said to believe and to repent (Article 12).

In the remainder of its consideration of the work of the Spirit in regeneration or the new birth, the Canons insist that the response of faith to the gospel is not a "work" in the power of the sinner either to accomplish or not. Faith is itself a "gift" of God, granted through the gospel by him "who works all things in all people." Nonetheless, God grants this gift of faith through the ministry of the gospel, so that the responsibility of the sinner is not denied but underscored. God does not treat those to whom the gospel call comes like "blocks or stones," abolishing their wills and coercing them to reply in faith. Through the ministry of the gospel, rather, God spiritually "revives," "heals," and "reforms" the sinner's will, granting to it a true freedom in readiness to do God's bidding.

Thus, the Canons conclude this fourth main point of doctrine by noting that God has in his good pleasure chosen to join inseparably the preaching of the gospel, the use of spiritual means, and the granting of faith to believers.

> Just as the almighty work of God by which he brings forth and sustains our natural life does not rule out but requires the use of means, by which God, according to his infinite wisdom and goodness, has wished to exercise his power, so also the aforementioned supernatural work of God by which he regenerates us in no way rules out or cancels the use of the gospel, which God in his great wisdom has appointed to be the seed of regeneration and the food of the soul (Article 17).

The Scriptural Support for This Position

There are several aspects to the Scripture's description of the work of the Spirit in the application of salvation that support this teaching of the Canons. I will mention four of them here.

In the first place, the Scriptures describe the Spirit's work in giving spiritual life and making believers God's children as a work of *regeneration* or *new birth*. In this granting of new birth to the believer, the Spirit makes sinners live spiritually, though they are in themselves dead in trespasses and sins. In this respect, the new birth may be likened to a resurrection from the dead or even a new act of creation.

The marvel of the Spirit's work of regeneration lies precisely in the fact that it is exclusively the Spirit's doing. No one, for instance, chooses to give himself birth. Just as our natural birth depends on the decision and will of others, so is the case of our spiritual birth. This is why we read in John 1:12, 13, "But as many as received Him, to them He gave the right to become children of God, even to those who believe in His name, who were born not of blood, nor of the will of the flesh, nor of the will of man, but of God." This is also the remarkable truth that Nicodemus, in his conversation with Christ, found initially so difficult to comprehend. As Jesus said to him, "Truly, truly, I say to you, unless one is born again, he cannot see the kingdom of God" (John 3:3). Only the Spirit of God is able to grant the new birth required to enter the kingdom of God (compare Titus 3:5; 1 Peter 1:23).

Similarly, the metaphors of new life and new creation underscore the surprising and sovereignly effective work of the Spirit in salvation. Just as death cannot give birth to life, so sinners cannot enliven themselves. And just as the act of creation calls into existence things that are not, so the Spirit creates anew in the act of salvation. In Ephesians 2:5, we read the following description of the new life in Christ: "Even when we were dead in our transgressions, [God] made us alive together with Christ (by grace you have been saved)" (compare Colossians 2:13). And in 2 Corinthians 5:17, we find a characteristic statement of salvation as the equivalent of a new creation: "Therefore, if any man is in Christ, he is a new creature; the old things passed away; behold new things have come" (compare Ezek. 36:26, 27; Gal. 6:15; Eph. 2:10).

In the second place, the Scriptures speak of the Spirit granting new sight to otherwise blind sinners through the revelation of the gospel. Whereas by nature we are blinded by sin and incapable of seeing the truth of the gospel, the Spirit opens our eyes through the Word to see the truth concerning our own sin and the glory of Christ. No more than a blind man can appreciate the light of day or the beauty of the sunset can a spiritually blind sinner appreciate the truth of the gospel. For this reason, the Spirit works through the gospel in such a way as to give sinners a true awareness of their needy condition and the remedy that is provided in the gospel (compare, for example, Luke 10:21; Eph. 1:17, 18). Only the Spirit of God is able to confirm to us the things of the Spirit. Therefore, those who do not have the Spirit illumining their minds cannot receive or approve of the message of the gospel. "But a natural man does not accept the things of the

Spirit of God; for they are foolishness to him, and he cannot understand them, because they are spiritually discerned" (2 Cor. 2:14).

In the third place, the Scriptures ascribe the acts of faith and repentance, by which sinners respond to the gospel call, to the Spirit who authors and gives them. Though faith and repentance are genuine acts, offered in response to the gospel, they are not independent acts, accomplished apart from the working of the Spirit. In the New Testament book of Acts, for example, there are several occasions where the faith and repentance of those to whom the gospel was preached are ascribed to God's working in the hearts of His people. In Acts 11:18, the believers in Jerusalem, on hearing of the repentance of the Gentiles at the preaching of the gospel, declare, "Well then, God has granted to the Gentiles also the repentance that leads to life." In Acts 13:48, when Paul announces the preaching of the gospel to the Gentiles, we are told that, "when the Gentiles heard this, they began rejoicing and glorifying the word of the Lord; and as many as had been appointed to eternal life believed" (compare Acts 5:31; Acts 16:14; Acts 18:27). Similar passages may also be found in the New Testament epistles, in which the faith and repentance of sinners are declared to be the gift of God (compare Eph. 2:8, 9; Phil. 1:29; 2 Tim. 2:25, 26).

And in the fourth place, the Scriptures often describe the call of the gospel as a sovereignly effective summons by which sinners are not only invited, but actually brought into the kingdom of God. The believer's calling through the gospel is not simply an "offer," which may or may not be answered. Rather, it is a gracious and sovereign act whereby the sinner is translated into the kingdom of God. This is the sense of Romans 8:30, where we read, "those whom . . . [God] predestined, these he also called; and those whom he called, these he also justified." Frequently, believers are simply identified by this calling; to be "called" is to be saved, numbered among the people of God (compare Rom. 1:6, 7; Rom. 9:23, 24; Gal. 1:15, 16;

1 Cor. 1:1ff; Jude 1:1; Rev. 17:14). In 2 Timothy 1:9, to be called and to be saved are used as synonyms: "God, who has saved us, and called us with a holy calling, not according to our works, but according to his own purpose and grace which was granted us in Christ Jesus from all eternity" (compare Heb. 9:15; 1 Peter 2:9; 1 Peter 5:10).

There is much more that could be said about each of these scriptural emphases. However, there should be no doubt that the work of God in the application of redemption is a sovereignly effective and irresistible work. How else could we interpret these scriptural comparisons, in which this work is likened to a new birth, a new creation, a new life, a new sight, and a new calling? In every one of these instances the Spirit works in us through the gospel what that gospel demands from us.

A Common Caricature

To conclude our consideration of the Canons' position on irresistible grace, there are two matters requiring further attention. The first concerns the manner in which the Canons are commonly caricatured. The second concerns the Canons' emphasis on the use of means in the Spirit's work in applying the gospel.

The common caricature to which I refer was one already made by the Arminians and addressed in the Canons themselves. This caricature says that the Reformed view the Spirit's work as "irresistible" in the sense that it entails an *overpowering* of the sinner's will, *coercing* the believer into the kingdom of God. Though it may be admitted that the language of "irresistible" grace could occasion this kind of caricature, this is nonetheless a distortion of the Canons' teaching.[2]

Since the authors of the Canons expressly answer this caricature, and do so in a way that cannot be easily surpassed, we do well to take heed to their words.

> Just as by the fall man did not cease to be man, endowed with intellect and will, and just as sin, which has spread through the whole human race, did not abolish the nature of the human race but distorted and spiritually killed it, so also this divine grace of regeneration does not act in people as if they were blocks and stones; nor does it abolish the will and its properties or coerce a reluctant will by force, but spiritually revives, heals, reforms, and—in a manner at once pleasing and powerful—bends it back. . . . It is in this that the true and spiritual restoration and freedom of our will consists. (Article 16)

The wonder of the Spirit's work is that He gives through the gospel the desire that alone gives birth to the deed. By means of the Spirit's gracious working in granting to sinners a new heart, there is granted a true freedom to will and to do, because this has become the desire of our hearts, what is in accord with God's own good pleasure.

The Use of Means

In the history of the Reformed churches, it has often been debated whether this regenerating work of the Spirit is "immediate" or "mediate." That is—does the Spirit grant the new birth through the use of the ministry of the gospel?

---

2. Perhaps it might be better to speak of "effectual grace." This captures the point well, and avoids the suggestion that believers are somehow compelled to enter the kingdom of God. It is important to note that the Scriptures do speak of those who willfully "resist" the Spirit of God (e.g. Acts 7:51), who refuse compliance with the demands of the gospel call to faith and repentance. This the Canons do not deny. In fact, they affirm as much when they speak of those who respond to the serious call of the gospel by spurning its promise and its demand.

Or—does the Spirit, in the strict sense, author this new birth without the use of the ministry of the Word? Some Reformed theologians have argued for the latter view, maintaining that the teaching of "mediate" regeneration imperils the exclusiveness of the Spirit's work in granting the new birth. These theologians fear that an emphasis on the use of means will detract from the truth that only the Spirit imparts new life.

However, it is clear from the Canons that the authors wanted to place the emphasis on the Spirit's use of the ministry of the gospel in bringing sinners to salvation. They wanted to stress the responsibility of the church to administer the gospel faithfully. And they insisted on the responsibility of those to whom the gospel call is extended to respond accordingly. Only within the setting of this administration of the gospel, comprising both the gospel call and the sinner's believing response, does God communicate His grace in Jesus Christ to believers.

This is a matter requiring our attention, because it belies the argument of many that the Canons' emphasis on the sovereign initiative and effective working of the triune God in the salvation of sinners belittles or diminishes human responsibility. This is clearly not the position of the Canons.

There is nothing in the Canons' description of the Spirit's working through the gospel that would diminish in any way the earnest, sincere, and serious proclamation of the gospel call to faith and repentance. There is nothing in the Canons' description of irresistible grace that would lessen in any degree the gospel summons to faith and repentance, together with the promise of salvation and blessedness to all who heed this summons. Nothing at all! Much rather there is every encouragement given to the ministry of the gospel, because it is by these means that sinners are brought into and kept within the kingdom of Christ.

In fact, as I suggested in an earlier chapter, such gospel preaching is not only encouraged by the confession of the Canons, it is also stimulated by the good confidence we may have that the Spirit will effectively use this gospel summons to bring believers to salvation. There need be no uncertainty or wishful thinking about the prospects of success when the gospel is preached according to the truth of the Scriptures. The wonderful confidence of gospel preaching, according to the Canons, is that God is pleased through these means to draw all His people without fail to Himself. None of those whom the Father has purposed to give to the Son, and for whom the Son laid down His life, will fail to be drawn by Him as the Spirit works effectively through the Word of the gospel.

Questions for Discussion

1. What is the relation between the teaching of "irresistible grace" and the other main points of doctrine of the Canons of Dort? Comment especially on the relation between "irresistible grace" and "total depravity."

2. Describe the harmony of the work of Father, Son, and Holy Spirit in the salvation of the believer.

3. Do you think it might be better to speak of "effectual grace" rather than "irresistible grace"? Why or why not?

4. What is the Arminian view of "resistible grace"?

5. How would you defend the teaching of "irresistible grace" against the conclusion that it means believers are saved "against their will"?

6. How does Jesus' teaching on the new birth in John 3:1–13 confirm the teaching on "irresistible grace" in the Canons of Dort?

7. What is meant by "mediate" or "immediate" regeneration? Consider James 1:18 and 1 Peter 1:23–25 in your answer.

Chapter Six

The Perseverance of the Saints

The Fifth Main Point of Doctrine

Throughout the foregoing discussion of the Canons of Dort, I have been emphasizing that they affirm two closely-related and fundamental themes of the gospel. These are: God's sovereign and gracious work in the redemption of His elect people, and the comfort this work affords the Christian believer. Only the gospel of God's free grace and mercy toward His beloved people, the bride whom He has purposed to give to Christ, His Son, and whom Christ purchased with His own precious blood, can steel the Christian believer for whatever he might face in life and death. Only this gospel provokes from the believer's lips the exclamation, "to God alone be the glory" (*soli Deo gloria*). Only this gospel grants the confident strength and expectation with which to face the present and the future.

When we come to the fifth main point of doctrine, the perseverance of the saints, these themes are once more on open display. Here the question is whether God, who has begun a good work of salvation in His people, is able and willing to bring it to completion. Is salvation truly God's work, His gracious doing, from its *conception* in His eternal counsel of election to its *consummation* in the glorification of the believer in the life to come? Is it God's work from beginning to end? After having confessed unconditional election, limited atonement (particular redemption), total depravity, and irresistible grace, the authors of the Canons were inevitably confronted with this matter of the believer's perseverance or continuance in a state of grace.

During the period prior to the convening of the Synod of Dort in 1618–1619, the Remonstrant or Arminian party in the Reformed churches of the Netherlands had concluded that there could be no certainty as to the believer's continuance in a state of grace. Even though in the fifth article of The Remonstrance of 1610 they had declined to commit themselves one way or the other on this point, by 1611 and the subsequent period leading up to the Synod of Dort, they had determined that there was no biblical warrant for affirming the perseverance of the saints.[1] They were unwilling to say that God unfailingly secures the redemption of the elect by enabling them to persevere in grace. Just as the believer's election depends on the conditions of foreseen faith and repentance, and on the believer's readiness to cooperate with (not resisting) the gracious working of the Spirit through the gospel, so the believer's perseverance depends on his own ability to continue in the course to the end.

The fifth main point of doctrine in the Canons of Dort provides quite a different answer to this question. Against the Remonstrant denial of the perseverance of the saints, the authors of the Canons affirmed that God sovereignly and graciously preserves those whom He has purposed to save. Salvation is God's doing—and that from beginning to end. Sovereign grace is the believer's comfort—and that both in life and in death.

The Position of the Canons

In the opening articles of the fifth main point of doctrine, the Canons of Dort acknowledge the presence and continuing conflict with sin in the life of true believers. Though

---

1. In the first chapter, introducing the Canons of Dort, I took note of this change in the position of the Remonstrants or Arminians on the fifth point of doctrine. Though the Remonstrants as late as 1610 still permitted a diversity of viewpoint on this subject, they drew the conclusion by the conference in The Hague in 1611 that it was unbiblical to teach that true believers must persevere in the way of salvation. It should be noted that this conclusion follows naturally from the Remonstrant positions on "conditional election" and "resistible grace." The "five points," whether in their Calvinist or Arminian form, do stand or fall together.

those whom God according to His purpose calls into fellowship with His Son, Jesus Christ, are delivered from the dominion of sin, they are not delivered "entirely from the flesh and from the body of sin" (Article 1). Believers continue to experience in this life "daily sins of weakness" and "blemishes" that cling even to the best of their works (Article 2). Such circumstances serve as an occasion for humility and a more earnest supplication of the help of the Spirit to remain on the course toward the goal of perfection. Indeed, it is even possible for believers to fall into serious sins, as was the case with David, Peter, and other saints described in the Scriptures. All of this ought to stimulate believers to constant watchfulness and prayer, and to a recognition that no one is so strong as to be incapable of falling into grievous sin.

It is within the setting of this biblically realistic view of the believer's daily and continual struggle with sin, that the authors of the Canons affirm the triune God's gracious preservation of the believer. Believers, were they left to their own resources, "could not remain standing in this grace" for a moment (Article 3). Only as God, being faithful and merciful, strengthens and enables them, are believers able to continue in that state into which God has brought them through fellowship with Christ. The good news of the gospel is not only that God has provided an atonement through Christ for us and brought us by the Spirit through the gospel into fellowship with Christ. But it is also that God remains faithful and merciful in preserving us within that fellowship.

> For God, who is rich in mercy, according to his unchangeable purpose of election does not take his Holy Spirit from his own completely, even when they fall grievously. Neither does he let them fall down so far that they forfeit the grace of adoption and the state of justification, or commit the sin which leads to death (the sin against the Holy Spirit), and plunge themselves, entirely forsaken by him, into eternal ruin (Article 6).

After acknowledging the believer's continuing weakness and liability to sin and affirming God's gracious intervention and preservation of the believer in the state of grace, the Canons highlight the comfort of this confession and the manner in which God provides for the believer's preservation.

The comfort of this confession resides in the certainty it grants of the believer's continuance in the way of salvation. Whereas the believer, left to himself, might easily stumble and fall irrevocably into sin, the preserving work of God in his life prevents this from occurring. The believer could no more fall out of favor with God and acceptance by Him than God's plan could change, His promise fail, His calling according to purpose be revoked, the merit of Christ nullified, and the sealing of the Spirit withdrawn (Article 8). Of this certain preservation believers have a right to be confident, not because of any "private revelation beyond or outside the Word, but from faith in the promises of God which he has very plentifully revealed in his Word for our comfort" (Article 10). And, though there may be seasons of doubt or wavering in this assurance, the Spirit rekindles the assurance of this preservation in us and employs it to provoke us to steadfast endurance in the Christian life. Contrary to the suggestion that the confidence of preservation will become the occasion for carelessness and indifference, it is an incentive that the Spirit uses to revive us in constancy and hope.

In their conclusion to this fourth main point of doctrine, the authors of the Canons focus their attention on the manner in which believers are preserved in a state of grace. Believers are *preserved* only as they *persevere* in the way of faith and obedience. This perseverance is itself stimulated and provoked by those means God is pleased to use to keep the believer on his gospel pilgrimage. These "means of grace" are the same as those God uses to produce faith.

> And, just as it has pleased God to begin this work of grace in us by the proclamation of the gospel, so he preserves, continues, and completes his work by the hearing and reading of the gospel, by meditation on it,

by its exhortations, threats, and promises, and also by the use of the sacraments (Article 14).

There is, accordingly, an intimate interplay between God's initiative and faithfulness in preserving the believer in fellowship with Christ and the believer's responsible use of those means God employs to enable him to persevere. God's gracious *gift* of preservation issues in and provokes the believer's responsible *task* of perseverance.

The Scriptural Support for This Position

It would be tempting at this point to argue simply that the perseverance of the saints follows inevitably from the other points of doctrine summarized in the Canons of Dort. For example, one could argue that God would surely not permit His purpose of election to be frustrated by the inability of the believer to stay the course. Or one could argue that the irresistible and sovereign work of the Spirit through the gospel could not be stymied (successfully resisted) down the way of the Christian's life, when a fall from grace occurred. However, it is not simply the illogic of the Remonstrant or Arminian position that counts against it, but its failure to do justice to the Scriptures.

There are several lines of scriptural support for the confession of the perseverance of the saints.

Kept by God's Power and Faithfulness

The first of these is Scripture's testimony to the power and faithfulness of God in keeping or preserving the believer in the way of salvation.

This testimony is found in a number of places. In 1 Corinthians 1:7–9, the apostle Paul expresses his confidence that the Lord will sustain the believers in Corinth "to the end, blameless in the day of our Lord Jesus Christ." The basis for his confidence is that "God is faithful, through whom you were called into the fellowship of his Son, Jesus Christ, our Lord" (compare 1 Cor. 10:13). In Jesus' high priestly prayer in John 17, it is noteworthy that He prays, "Holy Father, keep them in Thy name which Thou hast given me" (v. 11). This petition is then supported by Jesus' declaration that He has kept those whom the Father has given Him so that "not one of them perished" (v. 12).

This conviction that God will guard and keep His people, preserving them to the day of their full redemption and glorification, is also expressed in the salutations, concluding prayers, and benedictions of several New Testament epistles. Describing the believers to whom he writes, Jude begins with the greeting, "to those who are the called, beloved in God the Father and kept for Jesus Christ" (v. 1). This brief letter concludes with the benediction, "Now to Him who is able to keep you from stumbling, and to make you stand in the presence of His glory blameless with great joy . . . be glory, majesty, dominion and authority" (vv. 23, 24). In 1 Thessalonians 5:23, 24, the apostle Paul commends the believers to God's safekeeping, when he writes, "may your spirit and soul and body be preserved complete, without blame at the coming of our Lord Jesus Christ. Faithful is He who calls you, and He also will bring it to pass."

In these and other passages (e.g., 1 Peter 1:3–5), the believer's confidence of remaining in a state of grace and reaching the goal of his salvation is founded on God's power and faithfulness in keeping him.

Recipients of "Eternal Life"

It is also interesting to note that, in the Scriptures, the believer's fellowship with Christ through faith means an entrance into and experience of eternal life.

This can easily be shown from a number of familiar biblical passages. John 3:16, for example, declares that "God so loved the world that He gave his only begotten Son, that whoever believes in Him should not perish but have eternal life." In the following verses, Jesus announces that those who believe in the Son have eternal life already (v. 36; compare John 5:24; 6:47). In 1 John 2:19, 25, the apostle John sharply distinguishes those who are truly of Christ and those who are not; those who failed to remain with us prove, he asserts, that they were not truly of Christ. Those who are truly of Christ have the "promise which He Himself made to us: eternal life." It belongs to those who truly enjoy fellowship with the apostles, and thereby fellowship with Christ (1 John 1:3), that they continue steadfast in their profession (compare 1 John 5:4, 11–13, 20). The believer enjoys by faith the assurance of eternal life, a life that begins even now and never ends.

Because the believer has entered through faith into the enjoyment of eternal life, it is not surprising that the Scriptures often speak of future blessings as either virtually the believer's already or certain to be given. Believers who have been justified by the blood of Christ shall even more assuredly be saved by Him from the "wrath to come" (Rom. 5:8–10). Those who through faith are engrafted into Christ are no longer under condemnation (Rom. 8:1). For those whom God has called "according to His purpose," He has also justified and glorified (Rom. 8:35–39). Just as God has raised Christ from the dead, so He will not fail to "raise us also with Jesus and will present us with you" (2 Cor. 4:14). Believers who have died with Christ, and whose life is hid with Christ in God, will undoubtedly be given to "be revealed with Him in glory" (Col. 3:3, 4). In each of these respects, the believer's present possession in Christ is but a guarantee of that which will in the future be his in full measure.

Indwelt of the Holy Spirit

This emphasis on the believer's present enjoyment of eternal life and certainty of receiving in full in the future what he now enjoys only in part is also underscored by the biblical teaching that the Spirit who presently indwells the believer is a *seal* and *down payment* of full redemption.

The Holy Spirit, through whom we have communion with Christ, has been given to believers as a kind of "firstfruits" of that full harvest that will be given to the believer in the future. Thus, the apostle Paul can write in 2 Corinthians 5:5 that the Spirit is a kind of "down payment" on the believer's future enjoyment of imperishable life. Or he can speak of the believer's being "sealed with the promised Holy Spirit, which is the down payment of our inheritance until we acquire possession of it" (Eph. 1:13, 14; compare Eph. 4:30; Heb. 9:15).

In these passages, there is a clear and unbroken link between the believer's present enjoyment of the comfort of the indwelling Spirit and his future inheritance. The Holy Spirit's presence now is to the fullness of salvation in the future, what the first ingathering of the harvest is to the full ingathering. Not only is our present enjoyment of the Spirit *of a piece* with what will someday be ours in full, but it *guarantees* the believer's participation in that bountiful harvest.

Inseparable from God's Love

Consistent with these preceding lines of scriptural support for the perseverance of the saints, there is also the biblical theme of God's unfailing love in Christ for His people.

It is this unfailing love that undergirds the history of God's faithful and patient dealings with His covenant people (compare Isa. 54:10, "For the mountains may be removed and the hills may shake, but my lovingkindness will not be removed from you . . ." Jer. 32:40). It is this unfailing love that motivated Jesus Christ, the Good Shepherd, to lay down his life for His sheep and assure them that "no one shall snatch them out of My hand" (John 10:27–30; compare John 6:35–30). And it is this unfailing love that is celebrated in the well-known words of Romans 8:35, 37–39:

> Who shall separate us from the love of Christ? Shall tribulation, or distress, or persecution, or famine, or nakedness, or peril, or sword? . . . But in all these things we overwhelmingly conquer through him who loved us. For I am convinced that neither death, nor life, nor angels, nor principalities, nor things present, nor things to come, nor powers, nor height, nor depth, nor any other created thing, shall be able to separate us from the love of God, which is in Christ Jesus our Lord.

Once Saved, Always Saved

Before concluding our consideration of this fifth main point of doctrine, it is necessary to answer a common caricature of the perseverance of the saints. Though I have addressed in previous chapters other ways in which the teaching of the Canons is often caricatured, at no point is this more common or acute than in respect to the fifth point.

For example, I once heard a sermon by a televangelist who was criticizing the "five points of Calvinism." At one point in his sermon, the televangelist described what he regarded as the doctrine of the perseverance of the saints. He invited his listeners to imagine a view that teaches that anyone who professes to be a Christian cannot fall from grace. Imagine, he mockingly suggested, someone teaching concerning believers that "once saved, always saved." And he proceeded to describe a person who, though professing to believe and be a Christian, spent his life in an ungodly way. According to the teaching of the perseverance of the saints, this preacher alleged, this ungodly fellow would be safely ushered into heaven either at death or at Christ's return. The implication was clear—surely no one could seriously believe such a thing.

I mention this televangelist because his description of the doctrine of perseverance is a piece of fiction, bearing no relation to what the Canons set forth as the scriptural view. I also mention it because this misrepresentation of the doctrine was already being used by the Remonstrants and Arminians, when the Canons were first written.

What needs to be emphasized in reply to this misrepresentation is that the Canons speak of the *perseverance* of the *saints*. They affirm that those whom God preserves in the way of salvation, He preserves through the use of means by which believers persevere in faith, hope, and love. Consequently, the language used to describe this fifth main point of doctrine, "the perseverance of the saints," places considerable emphasis on the responsible use of those means God has given to produce and to preserve faith.

Not just anyone who professes to believe, however much he may deny this profession by an ungodly life, is said to be preserved in the way of salvation. Not at all. The Canons expressly reject this misunderstanding, and underscore the believer's responsible use of the means of grace as indispensable to his perseverance.

It is important to recognize this point, because some contemporary expressions of the doctrine of "eternal security" permit a kind of easy "once saved, always saved" complacency.[2] But this is not the doctrine of the Canons. In the Canons there is a strong insistence on the responsibility of the true believer to live a life worthy of his calling, persevering in faith and obedience, using every available means to be strengthened in the course.

The Faithfulness of Our Triune Redeemer

Lest I conclude on a defensive note, allow me once more to emphasize that it is the majesty and the splendor of our triune God's grace and faithfulness that is at stake in this part of the confession. The "God of all comfort, who comforts us in all our affliction" (2 Cor. 1:3, 4) is this God and Father of our Lord Jesus Christ. Not only has He loved us with a perfect love in Christ, from before the foundation of the world, without any merit or deserving on our part; not only has He granted us a perfect atonement for our sins through Christ's death; not only has He joined us in fellowship with Christ by the Spirit through the gospel—but He will always keep us in that perfect love.

One of the greatest errors anyone could commit would be to treat the confession given us in the Canons of Dort as though it were merely addressed to some fine point of doctrine, some hair-splitting but rather insignificant point. Nothing could be further from the truth. This confession deals with our knowledge of God as our sovereign Redeemer and of ourselves as poor and

---

2. In a subsequent chapter, I will address the contemporary significance of the Canons of Dort. In that chapter, I will have occasion to consider this counterfeit understanding of "eternal security" as it is expressed in some North American evangelical circles.

needy sinners. This confession deals with God's grace toward us in Christ, His invincible, surprising and matchless grace. This confession deals with our comfort for today and for tomorrow, in life and in death.

Allow me, then, to conclude with these stirring words from Article 15, the final article in this part of the Canons:

> This teaching about the perseverance of true believers and saints, and about their assurance of it—a teaching that God has very richly revealed in his Word for the glory of his name and for the comfort of the godly and which he impresses on the hearts of believers—is something that the flesh does not understand, Satan hates, the world ridicules, the ignorant and hypocrites abuse, and the spirits of error attack. The bride of Christ, on the other hand, has always loved this teaching very tenderly and defended it steadfastly as a priceless treasure; and God, against whom no plan can avail and no strength can prevail, will ensure that she will continue to do this. To this God alone, Father, Son, and Holy Spirit, be honor and glory forever. Amen.

Questions for Discussion

1. How is the teaching of the "perseverance of the saints" related to the other main points of doctrine of the Canons of Dort?

2. Why do you think the teaching of the "perseverance of the saints" is often so unpopular?

3. Why is it important to speak of the "perseverance of the *saints*"? What is the difference between speaking of the "perseverance" or the "preservation" of the saints?

4. Do the sins, even the serious falls (cf. King David, Peter), of the saints contradict the teaching of the "perseverance of the saints"?

Chapter Seven

The Canons of Dort and Reformed Evangelism

In several previous chapters, I have referred to the implications of the Canons' confession of God's sovereign grace in the salvation of His people for the preaching of the gospel today. However, these references were largely incidental to my purpose, which was to summarize the teaching of the confession and to show its biblical basis.

Having presented the historical background to the Synod of Dort and summarized the Canons' five main points of doctrine, I would like in this and subsequent chapters to address the issue of the significance of the Canons of Dort for today. How does this confession answer to the need of Reformed churches in their present circumstances?

It would be enough, of course, to argue that, because the Canons set forth biblical truth on the fundamental points of God's sovereign election and man's sinful, needy condition, they are inherently of abiding significance for the church of Jesus Christ. Since the Canons are addressed to that which is most basic to the gospel, it would be adequate to conclude simply that this is the message that the church of Jesus Christ must herald to the nations until Christ comes again. This gospel does not need to be made relevant; it is the only thing that answers to the sinner's need before the face of God.

However, it must be admitted that for many, even for some who call themselves "Reformed," the presumption is that the Canons have outlived their usefulness. Though they may be true, they do not address the questions of the present age. Furthermore, since they have a somewhat polemical cast, they do not serve the ecumenical objectives of an age that prefers peace to controversy and exalts tolerance as a virtue above commitment to the truth of God's Word. The Canons of Dort are an antiquated confession, arising out of particular circumstances and issues that the churches confronted in a bygone period. But they no longer speak in a fresh and compelling way to the needs of the contemporary church. For this reason, it becomes necessary to comment on what I regard to be the Canons' obvious significance for the church today.

A Hindrance to Evangelism?

One issue of compelling interest has to do with the significance of the Canons for the evangelistic calling of the church of Jesus Christ. As I have acknowledged in previous chapters, there have been many in the history of the churches who have argued that the Canons' emphasis on God's sovereign grace tends to undermine the urgency and impetus for the missionary calling of the church.

The argument goes something like this. If God is the sole Author of our salvation, if redemption is His work from first to last—He sovereignly elects, provides atonement through Christ, calls irresistibly through the gospel, and preserves the believer in the way of salvation—then there is no place for human responsibility. An emphasis on sovereign election leads inevitably to fatalism or passivism. To stress the invincible grace of God in the salvation of His people tends to minimize the indispensable place of the church in preaching the gospel to the lost and gathering them into the fellowship of Christ's church. If God will unfailingly secure the salvation of the elect, then the church is permitted to become complacent and inactive in the prosecution of her mission.

Though, as we shall see in a moment, this is a profound misunderstanding of the confession of God's sovereign grace, it must be admitted that some adherents of the Canons' teaching have lent support to this argument by adopting a passive and irresponsible approach to evangelism. I can recall well the comment of a parishioner in a Reformed congregation I served who lamented any sustained attention to and emphasis on the church's evangelistic calling by remarking, "but Pastor, the doors of our church are not closed; if anyone wants to come, he is free to come." The point of his remark, apparently, was that God would find a way to bring His own into the church and under the preaching of the gospel. But the church has no particular calling in this respect. The church does not have to instruct her members in the task of evangelism, or labor to bring the gospel to the lost. God would see to it that the elect were saved.

This argument—that the teaching of the Canons is a hindrance to evangelism—also appeals to their insistence that Christ died only for His own bride, not for all men without exception. As we saw in the chapter on "particular redemption," this, it is alleged, prevents the minister of the gospel from genuinely calling everyone to faith and repentance. The preaching of the gospel is unnecessarily cramped and limited in its application, since Christ's atoning work provides for the salvation of the elect alone. The evangelist, the preacher of the gospel, is therefore without authorization in saying to all men without distinction, "believe on the Lord Jesus Christ and you will be saved," or "God loves you, and Christ died for you."[1]

A Foundation for Reformed Evangelism

How shall we answer this objection? I believe we should answer it by insisting that the Canons, far from being a hindrance to evangelism, are an impetus to evangelism, but an evangelism of a distinctively Reformed type.

---

1. This was the argument of Professor Harold Dekker of Calvin Seminary in the so-called "love of God" controversy in the Christian Reformed Church in the 1960s. As I have previously noted, the first of these two declarations is biblical, the second is not.

Though it is true that some Reformed churches have been disobedient to their evangelistic calling (to their shame), it is not true that this disobedience is born out of their confession in the Canons. The reasons for the lethargy and passivity of some Reformed churches in respect to the task of evangelism are probably many.[2] It is not my purpose here to discover what they might be. But it is my purpose to defend the confession in the Canons from the false charge of those who would cite it as among those reasons.

In my judgment, the Canons provide an impetus for an evangelism that is Reformed (biblical) in its authorship, Reformed in its method, and Reformed in its aim.

Reformed in Its Authorship

When I say that the Canons provide for an evangelism that is Reformed in its authorship, I mean to emphasize that the work of evangelism is not first the church's or our work. It is the triune God's work. Typically, when we approach the subject of evangelism, preaching the gospel to the world and gathering Christ's flock, we take an activistic posture and approach. We act as though the triune God, Father, Son and Holy Spirit, has done His part, and now it falls to us to do what remains. God makes provision for the salvation of men; the church is called to do the saving.

At the risk of reinforcing the charge that Reformed believers are passive when it comes to the work of evangelism, I would insist that this is a profoundly unbiblical view of evangelism. Indeed, it is an Arminian view that threatens to restrict God to

---

2. Though it is permissible to look for a possible cause of this neglect of evangelism in the confessions of the Reformed churches, the connection needs to be demonstrated. In my judgment, the connection has not been demonstrated, and the reasons for some churches' neglect of the work of evangelism must be sought elsewhere. Moreover, it is not true that the Reformed churches throughout their history have been slack in fulfilling the Great Commission; many of them have been in the forefront of proclaiming the message of salvation to the nations.

the role of a hapless bystander or spectator in the salvation of His people.

Biblically speaking, we must always act out of the confidence, even boldness, of knowing that God the Father authored the evangelistic task of the church in His sovereign decision to save His elect; that God the Son provided a sure basis for the salvation of the elect in His perfect work of atonement; and that God the Holy Spirit invincibly applies that salvation to the hearts and minds of believers through the gospel. The triune God authors and effects salvation; the triune God therefore authors and effects the work of evangelism.

It is striking how this is underscored in the accounts in the book of Acts of the growth of the church after Pentecost.

At the end of Acts 2, in his description of the church in Jerusalem after Pentecost, Luke notes that "the Lord was adding to their number day by day those who were being saved" (v. 47). In Acts 6:7, it is the Word of the Lord that is said to "keep on spreading" so that the number of the disciples "continued to increase greatly in Jerusalem" (compare Acts 12:24, "But the Word of the Lord continued to grow and be multiplied"). When the apostle Peter reported to the church in Jerusalem the repentance and faith of the Gentiles, the church "glorified God, saying, 'Well then, God has granted to the Gentiles also the repentance that leads to life'" (Acts 13:18).[3]

This is the special contribution of the Canons of Dort to the church's understanding of her evangelistic task. Nowhere in the church's confessions do we find a more eloquent

---

3. Harry Boer, in his book, *Pentecost and Missions* (Grand Rapids, MI: Eerdmans, 1961), rightly argued that, in the book of Acts, the Holy Spirit is the primary Author of the evangelism of the church. The Great Commission, without the empowerment and working of the Spirit through the ministry of the Word, was not a sufficient basis for the church's mission. This is also well expressed in Lord's Day 21 of the Heidelberg Catechism: "That the Son of God, out of the whole human race, from the beginning to the end of the world, gathers, defends, and preserves for Himself, by His Spirit and Word, in the unity of the true faith, a Church chosen to everlasting life . . ."

affirmation of the great evangelistic work of our triune God who gathers His people to Himself through the ministry of the gospel of Jesus Christ.

Reformed in Its Method

I hasten, however, to add that this great work of evangelism, authored and effected by the triune God, is also the special responsibility and calling of the church of Jesus Christ. Christ gathers His people by His Spirit and Word in the unity of the true faith. Therefore, the church has been entrusted under Christ and empowered by the Spirit of Pentecost to discharge faithfully her stewardship of the gospel. To the whole church has been given the mandate to "go and make disciples of all nations" (Matt. 28:19; compare Mark 16:15), to preach repentance for the forgiveness of sins to all the nations (Luke 24:47). The triune God *uses means* to bring His people to salvation. And the church of Jesus Christ is, through the ministry of the gospel, the means He is pleased to use.

All of this has profound implications for the method of evangelism. If the work of evangelism is God's work, and if He is pleased to effect it through the ministry of the church, then the church must carry out her task in scrupulous conformity to God's chosen means. This is the great implication of God's authorship of the salvation of His people: evangelism must be done in accord with the design and pattern set down by God Himself.

In the Scriptures, it is clear that God is pleased to bring His people to salvation by means of the foolishness of the preaching (1 Cor. 1:18–25; 2:1–5). Not by might, not by power, but by the Spirit working through the Word does God give new birth to His people (James 1:18; 1 Peter 1:23–25). As the apostle Paul declares in Romans 1:16, "For I am not ashamed of the gospel, for it is the *power of God unto salvation* to everyone who believes, to the Jew first and also to the Greek." Or again, as he argues in Romans 10, "'Whoever will call upon the name of the Lord will be saved.' How then shall they call upon Him in whom they have not believed? And how shall they believe in Him whom they have not heard? And how shall they hear without a preacher? ... So faith comes from hearing, and hearing by the word of Christ" (vv. 13–14, 17).

Preaching the gospel of Jesus Christ, calling men and women to true faith and genuine repentance—this is the God-ordained instrument that is powerful to save all those whom Christ is gathering into the church. Though this might be foolishness and weakness to the world (also to the church to the extent that it has been intoxicated by the world), to the believer it is the wisdom and power of God.

Among many evangelical churches in North America, however, there has developed a kind of "method-ism" or fascination with a variety of strategies or devices thought to be useful to effect the salvation of the lost. Just as there is an Arminianism of confession, there is also an Arminianism of method. Because the salvation of people depends finally on some human power or means of persuasion, not the sovereign working of God through the gospel, methods have been devised that are accommodated to the desires and wishes of the natural man and are thought to hold greater promise of success than the simple preaching of the gospel to faith and repentance. Churches therefore are frantically casting about for some new method or approach that will prove more effective in gathering people into the fellowship of the church.

The only antidote to this Arminianism of method in evangelism is a Reformed evangelism that, rooted in a confession of God's sovereign grace, is content to carry out the task *in God's chosen manner.*

Reformed in Its Aim

Not only do the Canons remind of us of the true authorship and appropriate means of evangelism, but they also keep in proper perspective the aim or objective of biblical evangelism.

Reading many books on the subject and observing much of what is called "evangelism" in the churches today would suggest that the sole aim is to gather as many people as possible into the fellowship of local churches by whatever means seem to work. The primary, even exclusive, aim seems to be growth in numbers.

Now I do not wish to minimize the importance of "saving the lost" or reaching as many as possible with the gospel. Clearly, these are, in proper biblical perspective, legitimate aims of the church's evangelistic work. Christ Himself (and Paul, following his example) was clearly moved with compassion toward the multitudes who were like sheep without a shepherd (compare Matt. 10:36; Rom. 9:3). Christ's heart was not indifferent to the unbelief and impenitence of the people of Israel. Furthermore, the gospel makes clear that God's purpose includes the provision of an atonement for a great multitude who are being saved (Rev. 5:9). It is a misreading of Scripture to treat God's love for His people and provision in Christ for their redemption as though it were narrowly constricted in its extent. There is no place in Reformed churches for the idea that failure in gathering believers into the church is an evidence of faithfulness. Nor is there any place for churches composed of believers who are smugly content with the gospel "for themselves," but neglect to see to it that it is communicated to others. Nor is there place for a neglect of emphasis on the genuine growth of the congregation, both in numbers and in depth of knowledge and insight.

However, missing from much of the contemporary discussion and approach to evangelism is an emphasis on the chief, the primary aim—the glorification of God in the salvation and service of His people. This is why the end never justifies the means in evangelism. How is God glorified in an evangelism that minimizes the preaching of the whole gospel, the call to faith and repentance, and employs a laundry list of gimmicks and strategies that may be effective in drawing a crowd but woefully inadequate to the conversion of sinners? The purpose of evangelism is to gather men and women into the fellowship of the church, making disciples of the nations, bringing them under the dominion of Christ and His Word. And in such evangelism God is glorified; His saving grace is magnified; His kingdom comes.

Reformed evangelism, accordingly, always is careful to preach the gospel in the manner God has prescribed. It will never succumb to expediency in order to be "effective" in reaching large numbers, certainly not when this dishonors the majesty and glory of God.

What about "Seeker" Services?

To make more concrete the significance of the Canons for a Reformed approach to evangelism, one contemporary example of a non-Reformed and unbiblical approach may be useful.

Among the myriad of methods and devices fashioned by the modern evangelical church in North America to reach the lost, one of the more recent and influential is what is termed the "seeker service." Developed initially by Rev. Bill Hybels, pastor of one of the largest and most rapidly growing churches in America, this method uses a special service geared particularly, even exclusively, to the needs and circumstances of "seekers." "Seekers" are people who are not committed disciples of Jesus Christ and members of a local fellowship of believers. They may or may not be well acquainted with the teaching of the gospel or the Word of God. They are often distrustful of "organized religion," and may be turned off by the traditional ways of the church. Nevertheless, they are still open to the gospel and the ministry of the church to some extent; they are "seekers" who may be attracted to a special service of the church, provided it is especially sensitive to their needs and circumstances.

"Seeker's services," in this setting, are not worship services so much as special gatherings in which everything is done so as to present the gospel in a non-offensive or non-threatening fashion. The songs sung are typically contemporary choruses; the use of contemporary instruments, gospel singing troupes, and the like, is prevalent; "sermons" are not preached, but something called a "teaching" is presented; the "seeker" is not offended by being told he is a sinner in need of Christ, who must believe on His name and turn in repentance from sin; the sacraments are not administered; often evangelical celebrities are given a place of prominence; the service is offered at a convenient time and place; and every feature of the church's traditional worship that might be uncomfortable or difficult or liable to "turn off" the visitor is scrupulously avoided. This, in a general sort of way, is one of the newest methods being touted as an effective evangelistic tool.

What are we to make of this? Is this an approach that is in keeping with the evangelistic calling and work of the church of Jesus Christ?

In my view it is clearly not an approach that fits within the biblical and Reformed understanding of evangelism. However praiseworthy the motive and however legitimate the desire to remove any unnecessary obstacle to the hearing of the gospel, this method, like so many others, does not act in good biblical faith. That is to say, it does not proceed from the confident conviction that the triune God who is pleased to save His people is able and willing to do so only through the faithful ministry of the Word of the gospel. This approach substitutes for the preaching of the gospel the titillation and entertainment of the seeker. Or, to put it differently, this approach proceeds from the assumption that the seeker knows what he wants and needs, and it is the duty of the church to provide him the same.

However, in a biblically Reformed evangelism, the church proceeds on the assumption that only God knows the sinner's need and only God has provided an answer for that need. In a biblical setting, the church is never afraid to preach the gospel promiscuously to every one, with the same message and the same requirement of faith and repentance. Patiently, confidently, prayerfully—a Reformed church will preach the gospel. She will do so, without apology, knowing that God will achieve His saving purpose by these means—to His glory, not ours.

Recommended Reading:

Kuiper, R.B. *God-Centered Evangelism*. Grand Rapids, MI: Baker, 1961.

J.I. Packer. *Evangelism and the Sovereignty of God*. Downers Grove, IL: Intervarsity, 1961.

Questions for Discussion

1. Why does an emphasis on God's sovereign grace seem to many people to threaten an emphasis on the necessity of evangelism?

2. How would you defend the Canons of Dort against the claim that they remove any incentive for evangelism or preaching the gospel?

3. What contribution or implications do the Canons of Dort have for a Reformed approach to evangelism?

4. Describe and evaluate the modern "church-growth" movement. What are "seeker services"? Are they a biblical approach to worship and evangelism?

5. What explains the fact that Reformed believers and churches have often been reluctant to do the work of evangelism?

Chapter Eight

Sovereign Grace, Human Responsibility, and "Cheap Grace"

"What shall we say then? Are we to continue in sin that grace might increase? May it never be! How shall we who died to sin still live in it?" (Rom. 6:1–2).

As these well-known words of the apostle Paul imply, it is possible to conclude wrongly from the teaching that we are saved by grace alone that it doesn't matter then how we live. If God's grace fully answers to our need as sinners, if we do not have to add anything to it to complete our salvation, then we are free to revel in salvation as God's gift, without worrying about how we live in response to this gift. We can bask safely in the sunshine of God's favor and grace without having to live in obedience to His commandments. Indeed, we can continue to sin with impunity, knowing that this will only magnify the largeness of God's grace. The greater our sin, the greater God's grace.

Not only were there apparently some in the church at Rome who the apostle feared would wrongly draw this conclusion, but there have also been those who have done so throughout the history of the church. In the period of the Reformation, one of the most common complaints against the Reformers' teaching of salvation by grace alone was the alleged consequence of this teaching for the Christian life. Luther and Calvin were frequently charged with undermining any legitimate motive for or interest in pursuing a godly, sanctified life. After all—so it was alleged against their teaching—what good are good works if they do not purchase so much as an iota of our salvation?

If good works do not contribute anything, if they do not merit even the slightest part of our salvation, then the sinner will be inclined to sin that grace might abound.

This common complaint against the Reformers' teaching has also been leveled against the teaching of the Canons of Dort. Sometimes it takes a rather general form, and it is argued that God's sovereignty in grace is incompatible with an emphasis on human responsibility. At other times it takes a more specific form, and it is maintained that an emphasis on the sovereign grace of God makes the believer irresponsible and careless in the Christian life. Sovereign grace easily becomes cheap grace, a grace that comes free of charge and without any corresponding obligation to obedience.

Sovereign Grace and Human Responsibility

Most Reformed believers have a first-hand acquaintance with the argument that, to stress God's sovereign initiative and work in the salvation of His people threatens to undercut the need for a proper human response to the gospel. This argument was certainly prominent in the Arminian position, to which the Canons of Dort sought to provide a biblical answer.

In its extreme form, this argument likens the Canons' position on unconditional election, particular redemption, irresistible grace, total depravity, and the perseverance of the saints, to treating sinners like "blocks of wood" pushed and pulled about by God's sovereign will. In this caricature of the Canons, it is suggested that they teach a doctrine in which sinners are either compelled to enter or, alternatively, prevented from entering the kingdom, against their wills. Furthermore, sinners are kept within or excluded from the grace of God, regardless of their conduct or walk before the Lord. This reduces the role of the believer to that of a mere puppet in the hands of God.

Because the Canons ascribe the whole of our redemption to God's gracious initiative and provision in Christ, Arminians have insisted that they do not leave room for the free and lively involvement of sinners in their coming to and continuing in the way of salvation. In their view, unless God's election is conditional on the believer's own self-willed response to the call of the gospel to faith and repentance, for example, we cannot escape a kind of determinism that removes the seriousness of the gospel's call and undermines the responsibility of the believer.

What prevents, advocates of this claim ask, the Canons' insistence on God's sovereign election and grace from belittling the responsibility of sinners to answer the gospel call in faith and repentance? Doesn't this insistence reduce the believer's role to that of a passive bystander in the work of salvation? Just as the authors of the Canons feared the Arminian position would make God an inactive bystander at the critical juncture of the believer's response to the gospel, so the Arminians feared the Calvinist position would reduce the sinner to an inactive recipient of the grace of God.

The Charge of "Cheap Grace"

This argument often takes the specific form that an emphasis on sovereign grace cheapens the grace of God by treating it as though it were a gift, freely given and without strings attached. Since the whole of our salvation is God's doing, and since there is no place for merit in the obtaining of God's free gifts, there is really no incentive for responsible Christian conduct.

The authors of the Canons of Dort were well aware of this charge against their teaching. In the conclusion of the Canons, "Rejection of False Accusations," they acknowledge that there are those who insist

> that this teaching makes people carnally self-assured, since it persuades them that nothing endangers the salvation of the chosen, no matter how they live, so that they may commit the most outrageous crimes with self-assurance; and that on the other hand nothing is of use to the reprobate for salvation even if they have truly performed all the works of the saints.

This charge is really a different form of the issue considered in our previous chapter, whether an emphasis on the gracious work of God in the salvation of His elect people undermines the missionary activity and calling of the church.

Perhaps the force of this charge is best illustrated by a story told about a certain Lutheran minister of the gospel.[1] This minister of the gospel, when asked on his death bed whether he had the assurance of salvation, is said to have replied triumphantly, "Oh yes! I cannot remember ever having done a single good work!" The point of the story seems to be that an emphasis on salvation by grace alone is a kind of double-edged sword. On the one hand, it permits the believer to ground all of his confidence on God's grace alone, and not on his good works. And on the other hand, it removes any real urgency to live a life of good works. Why not sin, in order that grace may abound? Why not "sin boldly," even recklessly, since God's grace is freely given and freely received?

The "Lordship Salvation" Controversy

It is interesting to observe that a controversy has arisen among the evangelical churches in North America, sometimes termed the "lordship salvation" controversy, that has striking parallels with these historic debates about God's sovereign grace and human responsibility, particularly the debate whether sovereign grace cheapens the gospel's demand to respond in faith and repentance.

This "lordship salvation" controversy involves a dispute between those who advocate a radical doctrine of free grace and those who insist that God's grace does not remove, but accentuates, the responsibility of the believer to repent and live in obedience to God's commandments. Though this is not the place to provide a comprehensive summary and evaluation of this controversy, the respective positions taken in this controversy

---

1. Whether fictional or not, it is evident that this story has been told to illustrate the way an emphasis on free grace can be abused. Its use by critics of the Reformer's teaching resembles the way Luther's comment to Melanchthon, "sin boldly," has often been twisted to make Luther appear to have advocated a doctrine of "cheap grace."

serve to highlight the questions of divine sovereignty, human responsibility, and cheap grace.

On the one side of this controversy, there are those who advocate the position that grace is purely a gift, and may not be made "conditional" on the repentance of the sinner. Any language that treats repentance and submission to the lordship of Jesus Christ as an indispensable condition for the reception of the promise of the gospel and fellowship with God in Christ is regarded as a threat to the graciousness of God's grace. When repentance is treated as an inevitable and necessary component of any saving response to the gospel, then it becomes impossible to preserve the sovereignty of God's grace and the assurance that it gives. Any emphasis on the obligation to obey God's commandments, as an inseparable component of a saving response to the gospel call, is considered tantamount to a new form of salvation by works. This emphasis, moreover, robs the believer of his eternal security, the comfort that comes from receiving salvation as an irrevocable gift.[2]

On the other side of this controversy, there are those who advocate the position that, though grace is a gift freely imparted through the gospel, it demands the response of faith *and repentance*. Without a believing and obedient response to the call of the gospel, it is not possible to be saved. No believer may receive *Christ as Savior* without also receiving *Christ as Lord*. This position considers the first a form of "easy believism," in which the believer need only assent to the gospel promise without becoming subject to the lordship of Jesus Christ.

---

2. Many, though by no means all, of the advocates of this view are dispensationalists. The position takes various forms, one of which is to draw a sharp distinction between "carnal" and "spiritual" Christians, the former only acknowledging Christ as Savior, the latter also actively submitting to His lordship. The best representation of this view is given by Zane Hodges in the following: *The Gospel Under Siege: A Study on Faith and Works* (Dallas, TX: Redencion Viva, 1981); *Absolutely Free: A Biblical Reply to Lordship Salvation* (Dallas, TX: Redencion Viva, 1989; co-published and co-distributed by Zondervan).

This position also insists that the comfort of the gospel promise may not be treated in a presumptuous manner, as though God in the gospel throws a security blanket of acceptance over His people, irrespective of their perseverance in faith and repentance.[3]

While I do not wish to defend everything that has been written by those defending the second side of this controversy, it is apparent that the first side, the advocates of a radical doctrine of free grace, seems to have fallen prey to a view that diminishes human responsibility and threatens to cheapen the obligations of discipleship. And, since advocates of this view typically cite the Reformers' teaching of salvation by grace alone in their defense, it becomes necessary to ascertain whether their view is indeed in the line of the Reformation. Is it possibly the kind of position authorized by the Canons of Dort? Don't the Canons teach a similar view of the radical graciousness of the gospel promise and the eternal security that this promise grants to believers?

The Biblical Balance of the Canons

I have taken the trouble to summarize the usual form in which the position of the Canons is criticized, and provided a brief sketch of the present debate concerning "lordship salvation," to set the stage for evaluating the Canons' position. Do they emphasize divine responsibility at the expense of human responsibility? Do they give an occasion for a cheapening of the gospel obligations of faith and repentance? Furthermore, do they contribute anything to the dispute over "lordship salvation"?

To these questions I would answer that the Canons do present a biblically balanced view of divine sovereignty *and human responsibility*. They also vigorously oppose any misunderstanding of the working of God's grace through the gospel that would "cheapen" God's grace or diminish the

3. John MacArthur defends this position and critically evaluates the former position in his *The Gospel According to Jesus* (Grand Rapids, MI: Zondervan, 1988). Though he defends a premillennial dispensationalist eschatology, MacArthur attempts to affirm both God's sovereign grace in salvation and the indispensable conditions of discipleship in the Christian life.

necessity of a responsible perseverance in the way of obedience to the gospel.

Responsibility to the Grace of God

To appreciate the Canons' biblical balance on the relation between God's sovereign grace and human responsibility, it is important to remember that the Canons are, by their own admission, a somewhat one-sided and focused summary of biblical teaching. The authors of the Canons did not intend their confession to provide a complete summary of biblical teaching, in the way that the Belgic Confession and other Reformation confessions do, for example. Their focus was dictated by the five points of doctrine of the Remonstrants or Arminians. Since the Remonstrant position diminished the sovereign grace of God as the single foundation of the salvation of His people, the authors of the Canons were obliged, in defense of the Scripture's teaching of unconditional election, to accentuate the graciousness of God in saving His people. The vigor and force of the Canons' affirmation of the triune God's initiative and sovereign provision of salvation for His people can only be understood against the background of the crisis among the Reformed churches brought about by the Arminian party. The grand theme of the Reformation's rediscovery of the gospel—*sola gratia*, "by grace alone"—was at stake.

It is all the more remarkable, then, that the Canons, though vigorously defending the sovereign grace of God at every point it faced attack, refused to succumb to the kind of determinism described earlier. They simultaneously affirm *unconditional election* (those only are saved whom the Father elected in Christ from before the foundation of the world) and *conditional condemnation* (those only are condemned who have sinned in Adam and refused to serve God in faith and repentance). They simultaneously teach particular redemption (Christ provided atonement for those whom the Father purposed to give to Him) and universal gospel preaching (seriously calling all men, without exception, to faith and repentance, promising life to all who respond accordingly). They simultaneously insist on the sinner's total depravity (his inability to answer the gospel call in his own strength) and the sinner's real obligation to respond to the gospel's call to faith and repentance. They simultaneously speak of God's gracious *preservation* of His people in the way of salvation and His people's urgent *perseverance* in the way of salvation.

Now to some this may only seem to be a series of paradoxes, even contradictions. How may we simultaneously affirm what appear to be a series of contrary teachings? However, as G. K. Chesterton, the well-known English writer, once remarked, a paradox may only be "the truth stood on its head to gain our attention." A paradox need not be an actual contradiction. A paradox might be, as is the case with the Canons, a deliberate holding to both sides of the biblical truth without letting go of either and thus losing one's balance. This is precisely what we have in the Canons: the authors refused to lose their biblical balance, even when faced with the Arminian challenge. They were willing to hold tenaciously to both sides of the biblical picture, divine sovereignty and human responsibility, without falling prey to the temptation of resolving the apparent contradiction in favor of one side or the other.

This is the strength of the Canons' testimony to God's sovereign grace. The authors of the Canons were willing to live with the *apparent* conflict or tension between these two biblical emphases, but refused to grant that this conflict was *real*. They were willing to follow the Scriptures wherever they led, leaving to the triune God the resolution of what within His counsel must be a perfect consistency and harmony. In so doing, they are the model of humility in summarizing the total teaching of Scripture, leaving to God the resolution of these differing emphases. They stand in marked contrast to the rationalism of the Arminian position which, in order ostensibly to protect human responsibility, compromises the clear biblical testimony to God's sovereign grace.

Costly Grace

Consistent with their simultaneous emphasis on God's sovereign grace and the responsibility of the believer to answer to that grace in faith and repentance, the Canons resist every attempt to "cheapen" the grace of God. This is evident in at least two important ways.

First, though the grace of God in Christ is freely given to the elect, this grace exacted an infinite cost of Christ through His atoning work. Whenever we affirm that salvation is God's free gift, an expression of His sovereign and boundless mercy toward His people in Christ, we may not forget that it is a salvation purchased for us through Christ's work of satisfaction on our behalf. As the Canons describe it, "This death of God's Son is the only and entirely complete sacrifice and satisfaction for sins; it is of infinite value and worth, more than sufficient to atone for the sins of the whole world" (Second Main Point of Doctrine, Article 3).

This means that, though the Canons resolutely oppose any hint of human merit or works done to satisfy God's justice and purchase our salvation, the grace of God is always a costly grace. It may be freely given to the believer, but it was not purchased without the price of the precious blood of the Savior. God the Father does not relinquish His holiness or righteousness in granting salvation to the elect. He satisfies His own holiness in the satisfaction made through the atoning work of His Son. Those who too quickly complain against the Canons' insistence on the free and sovereign grace of God toward His elect in Christ often neglect to acknowledge this.

Here the Canons offer a similar reply to that Calvin offered to those who complained that he offered God's grace too cheaply to sinners. Though the gospel freely promises salvation to those who accept this promise with a believing heart, this does not mean the gospel comes cheap. As Calvin retorted to his critics, the grace of God purchased for us by Christ comes at a much higher cost than the pittance of any of our supposed "satisfactions."

Second, in their description of the believer's perseverance in the way of salvation, the Canons provide absolutely no room for the idea of cheap grace, as we have described it in the foregoing. Not only do the Canons use language, "perseverance," that places a great deal of emphasis on the believer's responsibility to work out his salvation with fear and trembling, but they also characterize this perseverance in terms that clearly resist the idea that the believer could trifle with the promise of God or seize on it as an occasion to sin.

There is, in this respect, a decided difference between the Canons' teaching of perseverance and what often today is meant by "eternal security." Whereas the language of "eternal security" suggests a safe haven of inactivity and passive receiving of God's promise, the language of the Canons suggests a dynamic walk in communion with the Lord, marked by a diligent use of the means of grace and response to the admonitions and warnings of the gospel to stay the course. The former language intimates that the Christian life is akin to resting in a gift received; the latter intimates that the Christian life is akin to a marriage relationship, in which husband and wife pledge to walk with each other in "constant faithfulness and abiding love."

Therefore, no one who reads the Canons of Dort carefully and appreciatively should conclude that they, by exalting God's sovereignty, diminish human responsibility. This is a false dilemma that the framers of this confession studiously avoided, even at the risk of being charged with inconsistency. Furthermore, no one should confuse their emphasis on God's sovereign grace with any doctrine of cheap grace. God's sovereign grace works in the life of the believer to produce the obedience of faith and repentance at the preaching of the gospel. It is granted to those alone who receive it in faith and repentance, acknowledging Christ as Savior *and Lord*. There is no place, then, in this confession for "easy believism" or an irresponsible use of the gospel.

Questions for Discussion

1. What is meant by "cheap grace"? Why is "cheap grace" so often linked with "sovereign grace"?

2. What is meant by "lordship salvation" and "non-lordship salvation"?

3. Why can believers not have Christ as their "Savior," unless He is also their "Lord"?

4. How would you describe the relation between justification and sanctification in the life of the believer?

5. What is meant by the "biblical balance" of the Canons of Dort?

Chapter Nine

Concluding Observations

Now that we have come to the end of our journey through the Canons of Dort, it is time to draw some conclusions regarding their continued usefulness and importance for the Reformed churches today. This will enable us to tie up some remaining loose threads in the previous chapters, and to underscore what has been one of my major theses throughout: Reformed believers need to rediscover and benefit from their rich confessional inheritance in the Canons of Dort. Though often neglected and misunderstood, as we have seen, this confession of faith has much to contribute to the life and ministry of the church.

Unswervingly Biblical

The first observation concerns the unswervingly biblical character of this confession of faith.

In the *Westminster Confession of Faith*, a Reformed confession that comes from a period of history and an ecclesiastical context in many ways different from that which occasioned the Synod of Dort in 1618–1619, there is a beautiful statement of the Reformed view of the supreme authority of the Word of God in determining the truth. Found in the first chapter, Article X, this statement declares that

> the supreme judge by which all controversies of religion
> are to be determined, and all decrees of councils, opinions
> of ancient writers, doctrines of men, and private spirits,

are to be examined, in whose sentence we are to rest, can be no other but the Holy Spirit speaking in Scripture.

When the dispute over election arose in the Reformed churches in the Netherlands in the late sixteenth and early seventeenth centuries, the earliest debate focused on Article XVI of the Belgic Confession. Does this article truly express the scriptural teaching of God's sovereign, unconditional election of His people in Christ? Or, is it an unscriptural article of faith? When Arminius challenged the confession of election in the Reformed churches, his challenge required the Reformed churches to determine whether their confession was based on the Word of God. The Reformed churches were confronted with a test case, in other words, as to whether they were willing to live by their own confession of the supreme authority of the Word of God.

It has been the burden of my argument in the preceding chapters to demonstrate how, on each contested point of doctrine, the Canons admirably meet this test. Without swerving either to the left or to the right, the Canons consistently adhere to the line of biblical truth.

Since the Scriptures teach that God elects His people to salvation by grace alone, and not on the condition of foreseen faith and repentance, the Canons confess this truth. Since the Scriptures teach that some, though not all, are chosen, while others are passed by in God's electing purpose, the Canons affirm particular election as well as non-election. When the Arminians alleged that this would make God the Author of sin and unbelief or undermine the serious call of the gospel, promising life and salvation to everyone who believes, the authors of the Canons steadfastly refused to draw this conclusion. Why? Because the Scriptures teach both particular election and a universal gospel summons. That the Scriptures teach both was enough, and so both found their echo in the affirmations of the Canons.

Similarly, since the Scriptures teach that Christ's work of atonement was provided on behalf of those whom the Father purposed to save and give to Him, the Canons resist the Arminian view that the universal summons of the gospel requires a universal atonement. And, since the Scriptures teach the preservation of the believer in the way of salvation and the urgent obligation to persevere in the way, the Canons likewise affirm both emphases with equal vigor.

Many more examples of the scriptural faithfulness and balance of the Canons could be cited. What is remarkable is how the Canons consistently resist the temptation of rationalism. Rationalism, or the reliance on human reason competently to determine and measure the truth without being submissive to the Scriptures, more than meets its match in this confession. Without attempting to delve into the mystery of God's electing purpose beyond the boundaries of scriptural revelation, and without attempting to effect an easy resolution of biblical emphases that may appear to us incapable of harmonization, the Canons follow the Scriptures wherever they lead, while refusing to go further than the Scriptures go. In so doing they are a model of the Reformation's commitment to *sola Scriptura*; by the standard of the Word of God alone we are to judge and determine what is true.

A One-Sided/Focused Confession?

A second observation regarding the Canons of Dort relates to what might be termed the one-sidedness or specific focus of this confession.

In a previous chapter, I referred to this feature of the Canons, when I observed that they address one particular aspect of Scripture's teaching that was being contested among the Reformed churches of the Netherlands in the post-Reformation period. It was not the purpose of the authors of the Canons to provide a comprehensive statement of scriptural teaching in the same fashion as a confession like the Belgic Confession or the Heidelberg Catechism or the Westminster Confession of Faith. The focus of the dispute in the Netherlands was quite limited; it had to do with the confession of election, particularly whether this election was in any way founded on the condition of faith in the gospel.

This historical occasion and limited focus of the dispute among the Reformed churches in the Netherlands are often forgotten by critics of the Canons, when they charge them with narrowing the scope of the Reformed faith. It is simply unfair to compare the Canons directly with the broader and more wide-ranging confessions of the Reformation period, or to judge that they have inappropriately narrowed the focus of an earlier Reformed or Calvinistic "world and life view" by reducing the compass of the Reformed faith to what are sometimes termed the "doctrines of grace." Such criticism neglects to appreciate the deliberate focus and acknowledged limitation of this confession of faith. The Canons were never intended to serve the churches as a substitute for the more full confession of faith provided in the other creeds. They were intended to supplement and clarify the Reformed faith at precisely that critical point where this faith was being severely tested.

Perhaps this can be illustrated by considering a picture of a landscape scene that encompasses a wide panorama within its range of vision. Such a landscape could be surveyed or viewed in its broadest possible scope. However, it would be possible to fix one's attention or sight on an object that, on closer scrutiny, has a central place and prominence in the landscape. If one looks at the landscape comprehensively, this item might escape initial notice. However, if one examines the landscape more carefully, this otherwise unnoticed item comes into bold relief.

Something like this is true of the broad confession of faith, or world and life view, that Reformed Christianity or Calvinism represents. Seen comprehensively, it covers a range of vision that cannot be limited to the biblical teaching concerning election.[1] It includes a perspective not only on the life and ministry of the church, but also on: the vocation or calling of God's people to exercise a responsible stewardship of God's gifts, the civil order and task of the magistrate, the ordering of a just economy, an approach to Christian scholarship in the academy, and the like. The Reformed faith is as broad as the biblical faith, comprising the whole of God's revelation of Himself in the creation of the world, the redemption of His people, and the consummation of His kingdom.

The Canons represent what lies at the heart of the Reformed world and life view, namely, the sovereign initiative and grace of God in the restoration of a people to communion with Himself and to the glorification and service of His great name. But they do not encompass the whole of this world and life view. Consequently, when the Canons are evaluated, they should not be charged with restricting the compass of the Reformed faith too narrowly. They do not claim to set forth the whole of the Reformed faith. Nor do they claim to provide the answer to questions to which they are not addressed. They aim only to confess salvation by grace alone in terms of the biblical teaching of election. With respect to this aim, they are on target.

A God-Centered Faith

Perhaps the most important reason the Canons of Dort are not as popularly known or appreciated as they should be, has to do with their God-centeredness. Or, to state the matter negatively, because the Canons of Dort are anti-humanistic through and through, they do not find a congenial home in an

---

1. See H. Henry Meeter, *The Basic Ideas of Calvinism* (6th ed.; Grand Rapids: Baker Book House, 1990), for a readable and concise statement of a Calvinistic world and life view. Meeter argues that the sovereignty of God is the "basic principle" of Calvinism. Though this principle comes to magnificent expression in the doctrine of election, this doctrine, while expressive of what might be termed "soteriological Calvinism," does not comprehend the whole of Calvinism's application of this principle.

age that has inherited an Enlightenment spirit that emphasizes man's autonomy and liberty.

It is not possible to underestimate the extent to which the spirit of the Enlightenment has made its inroads in Western culture and societies, and as well in the churches. This spirit chafes under the biblical teaching that all men are constituted sinners in Adam, born and conceived in sin, worthy only of condemnation and death. The biblical teaching that all men are wholly incapable of doing any saving good—spiritually blind to the truth of God's Word, spiritually enslaved to the dominion and principle of sin, spiritually dead in trespasses and sins—is regarded by many as an intolerable assault on the dignity of man and his place under the sun.

Furthermore, it is regarded as sacrilege that man should not be free to determine his own destiny, to "pull himself up by his own bootstraps," and to forge for himself a future of his own making. If God should have any role to play in all this, it can only be that of a co-laborer or fellow-traveler, not that of the sovereign Creator and Lord of history who administers all things in accordance with His holy will (Eph. 1:11). If credit is to be assigned, God will receive His due, but only if He is regarded as One who helps us along the way but leaves to us the initiative in beginning as well as finishing the course.

Sadly, this spirit also enjoys a warm reception within many churches. In an age of "consumer religion," which tailors the gospel to the tastes of the religious public, many of the biblical notes sounded in the Canons of Dort are muted at best, wholly silenced at worst. In an age devoted to "church growth," not so much by the simple preaching of the biblical gospel, calling sinners to true faith and genuine repentance, but to those methods that will attract a crowd and garner the most traffic, the sober emphases of the Canons do not appear particularly attractive. Won't the preaching of sin and grace be too threatening to many contemporary seekers? Won't the gospel summons to repentance put off more than it attracts? Won't the emphasis on God's gracious provision for needy sinners through the atoning work of Christ and the working of the Spirit through the gospel tend to displace and diminish the religious desires and interests of many contemporary people?

I raise these questions to illustrate again how different is the emphasis and approach of the Canons to the proclamation of the gospel. According to the Canons, the chief end and fruit of all gospel preaching is the glorification of the living God, the triune Creator and Redeemer. The first, middle, and last word of this confession of faith addresses the reality of the triune God's gracious initiative, provision, application, and preservation of His people in the way of salvation in Christ. This confession does not speak, first, of man and his aspirations for God, but of God and His free decision to choose a people whom He gives to Christ, His Son. This is a confession that speaks, not of man's initiative and action, but of God's. It is a confession that begins and ends, celebrating the grandeur of God in His sovereign purposes and works, whether in the merciful election of His people or the just condemnation of the sinful and unbelieving.

The "God of All Comfort"

In his second letter to the church in Corinth, the apostle Paul blesses God by saying, "Blessed be the God and Father of our Lord Jesus Christ, the Father of mercies and God of all comfort; who comforts us in all our affliction . . ." (2 Cor. 1:3–4). In this blessing, the apostle describes the God and Father of our Lord Jesus as the "God of all comfort," as the One who encourages and sustains the believer in all circumstances.

A sympathetic reader of the Canons of Dort will notice that this too lies at the heart of this Reformed confession: only the Father who sovereignly elects His people in Christ, His Son, can provide the comfort, the solid joy and lasting treasure sinners need. Were the believer to find his comfort in his own faith, in his own "choice" for God, in his own ability to continue to run the race with perseverance—what an empty comfort or consolation this would be. Believers who know themselves in the light of the Word of God have no desire to place their hope and prospect for salvation in their own hands. Much better to place their hope in the capable and faithful hands of God the Father who, for the sake of Christ, His Son, will permit nothing to snatch His people from His hands (John 10:28).

Here it needs to be observed that the Canons' God-centeredness does not diminish their comfort. For the believer's true comfort resides not in himself but in His God. When our salvation is made to depend, even in the slightest measure, on our own initiative and persistence in the course, it hangs not from the thinnest of threads but from nothing at all. Nothing could more certainly steal from the believer his hope and confidence, whether in this life or the life to come, than to rest on or place his trust in his own resources, pluck, or self-determination. The only solid comfort, by comparison, is to be found in God the Father's gracious election of His people, God the Son's perfect provision and atonement on their behalf, and God the Spirit's calling them into and preserving them in fellowship with Christ through the gospel.

The God-centeredness and solid comfort of the Canons, then, are two sides of a single coin. Calvin was correct when he opened his *Institutes* by remarking that all Christian wisdom is comprised of the knowledge of God and the knowledge of ourselves. The one always influences and shapes the other. What we believe concerning God has everything to do with what we know about ourselves. What we know about ourselves must derive from what we know of God. Consequently, when Reformed believers confess that the God and Father of our Lord Jesus Christ has loved His own with a perfect love from all eternity, they seek to live to the praise of His matchless grace, knowing that in Him they have the fullness of joy.

The authors of the Canons understood this correspondence between emphasizing God's sovereign grace and finding solid comfort in the gospel. They remind us of it in the words of their conclusion:

May God's Son Jesus Christ, who sits at the right hand of God and gives gifts to men, sanctify us in the truth, lead to the truth those who err, silence the mouths of those who lay false accusations against sound teaching, and equip faithful ministers of his Word with a spirit of wisdom and discretion, that all they say may be to the glory of God and the building up of their hearers. Amen.

Questions for Discussion

1. How do the Canons of Dort remind us of the importance of being "unswervingly biblical" in all of our teaching and preaching?

2. Why is it so important to remember the historical situation in which the Synod of Dort met and the Canons of Dort were written?

3. The Canons of Dort are God-centered; they focus on what God does in the salvation of His people. Is this emphasis typical in the churches today? Defend your answer.

4. How does the teaching of the Canons of Dort comfort believers?

The Canons of Dort

Formally Titled
The Decision of the Synod of Dort
on the Five Main Points of Doctrine
in Dispute in the Netherlands

The First Main Point of Doctrine

Divine Election and Reprobation

The Judgment Concerning Divine Predestination
Which the Synod Declares to Be in Agreement with the Word of
God and Accepted Till Now in the Reformed Churches, Set Forth
in Several Articles

Article 1: *God's Right to Condemn All People*
Since all people have sinned in Adam and have come under the
sentence of the curse and eternal death, God would have done no one
an injustice if it had been his will to leave the entire human race in sin
and under the curse, and to condemn them on account of their sin.
As the apostle says: *The whole world is liable to the condemnation
of God* (Rom. 3:19), *All have sinned and are deprived of the glory
of God* (Rom. 3:23), and *The wages of sin is death* (Rom. 6:23).*

---

*All quotations from Scripture are translations of the original Latin
manuscript.

Article 2: *The Manifestation of God's Love*
But this is how God showed his love: he sent his only begotten Son into the world, so that whoever believes in him should not perish but have eternal life.

Article 3: *The Preaching of the Gospel*
In order that people may be brought to faith, God mercifully sends proclaimers of this very joyful message to the people he wishes and at the time he wishes. By this ministry people are called to repentance and faith in Christ crucified. For *how shall they believe in him of whom they have not heard? And how shall they hear without someone preaching? And how shall they preach unless they have been sent?* (Rom. 10:14–15).

Article 4: *A Twofold Response to the Gospel*
God's anger remains on those who do not believe this gospel. But those who do accept it and embrace Jesus the Savior with a true and living faith are delivered through him from God's anger and from destruction, and receive the gift of eternal life.

Article 5: *The Sources of Unbelief and of Faith*
The cause or blame for this unbelief, as well as for all other sins, is not at all in God, but in man. Faith in Jesus Christ, however, and salvation through him is a free gift of God. As Scripture says, *It is by grace you have been saved, through faith, and this not from yourselves; it is a gift of God* (Eph. 2:8). Likewise: *It has been freely given to you to believe in Christ* (Phil. 1:29).

Article 6: *God's Eternal Decision*
The fact that some receive from God the gift of faith within time, and that others do not, stems from his eternal decision. For *all his works are known to God from eternity* (Acts 15:18; Eph. 1:11). In accordance with this decision he graciously softens the hearts, however hard, of his chosen ones and inclines them to believe, but by his just judgment he leaves in their wickedness and hardness of heart those who have not been chosen. And in this especially is disclosed to us his act—unfathomable, and as merciful as it is just—of distinguishing between people equally lost. This is the well-known decision of election and reprobation revealed in God's

Word. This decision the wicked, impure, and unstable distort to their own ruin, but it provides holy and godly souls with comfort beyond words.

Article 7: *Election*
Election [or choosing] is God's unchangeable purpose by which he did the following:

> Before the foundation of the world, by sheer grace, according to the free good pleasure of his will, he chose in Christ to salvation a definite number of particular people out of the entire human race, which had fallen by its own fault from its original innocence into sin and ruin. Those chosen were neither better nor more deserving than the others, but lay with them in the common misery. He did this in Christ, whom he also appointed from eternity to be the mediator, the head of all those chosen, and the foundation of their salvation.

> And so he decided to give the chosen ones to Christ to be saved, and to call and draw them effectively into Christ's fellowship through his Word and Spirit. In other words, he decided to grant them true faith in Christ, to justify them, to sanctify them, and finally, after powerfully preserving them in the fellowship of his Son, to glorify them.

God did all this in order to demonstrate his mercy, to the praise of the riches of his glorious grace.

As Scripture says, *God chose us in Christ, before the foundation of the world, so that we should be holy and blameless before him with love; he predestined us whom he adopted as his children through Jesus Christ, in himself, according to the good pleasure of his will, to the praise of his glorious grace, by which he freely made us pleasing to himself in his beloved* (Eph. 1:4–6). And elsewhere, *Those whom he predestined, he also called; and those whom he called, he also justified; and those whom he justified, he also glorified* (Rom. 8:30).

Article 8: *A Single Decision of Election*
This election is not of many kinds; it is one and the same election for all who were to be saved in the Old and the New Testament. For Scripture declares that there is a single good pleasure, purpose, and plan of God's will, by which he chose us from eternity both to grace and to glory, both to salvation and to the way of salvation, which he prepared in advance for us to walk in.

Article 9: *Election Not Based on Foreseen Faith*
This same election took place, not on the basis **of** foreseen faith, of the obedience of faith, of holiness, or of any other good quality and disposition, as though it were based on a prerequisite cause or condition in the person to be chosen, but rather for the purpose of faith, of the obedience of faith, of holiness, and so on. Accordingly, election is the source of each of the benefits of salvation. Faith, holiness, and the other saving gifts, and at last eternal life itself, flow forth from election as its fruits and effects. As the apostle says, *He chose us* (not because we were, but) *so that we should be holy and blameless before him in love* (Eph. 1:4).

Article 10: *Election Based on God's Good Pleasure*
But the cause of this undeserved election is exclusively the good pleasure of God. This does not involve his choosing certain human qualities or actions from among all those possible as a condition of salvation, but rather involves his adopting certain particular persons from among the common mass of sinners as his own possession. As Scripture says, *When the children were not yet born, and had done nothing either good or bad . . . , she* (Rebecca) *was told, "The older will serve the younger." As it is written, "Jacob I loved, but Esau I hated"* (Rom. 9:11–13). Also, *All who were appointed for eternal life believed* (Acts 13:48).

Article 11: *Election Unchangeable*
Just as God himself is most wise, unchangeable, all-knowing, and almighty, so the election made by him can neither be suspended nor altered, revoked, or annulled; neither can his chosen ones be cast off, nor their number reduced.

Article 12: *The Assurance of Election*

Assurance of this their eternal and unchangeable election to salvation is given to the chosen in due time, though by various stages and in differing measure. Such assurance comes not by inquisitive searching into the hidden and deep things of God, but by noticing within themselves, with spiritual joy and holy delight, the unmistakable fruits of election pointed out in God's Word—such as a true faith in Christ, a childlike fear of God, a godly sorrow for their sins, a hunger and thirst for righteousness, and so on.

Article 13: *The Fruit of This Assurance*

In their awareness and assurance of this election God's children daily find greater cause to humble themselves before God, to adore the fathomless depth of his mercies, to cleanse themselves, and to give fervent love in return to him who first so greatly loved them. This is far from saying that this teaching concerning election, and reflection upon it, make God's children lax in observing his commandments or carnally self-assured. By God's just judgment this does usually happen to those who casually take for granted the grace of election or engage in idle and brazen talk about it but are unwilling to walk in the ways of the chosen.

Article 14: *Teaching Election Properly*

Just as, by God's wise plan, this teaching concerning divine election has been proclaimed through the prophets, Christ himself, and the apostles, in Old and New Testament times, and has subsequently been committed to writing in the Holy Scriptures, so also today in God's church, for which it was specifically intended, this teaching must be set forth—with a spirit of discretion, in a godly and holy manner, at the appropriate time and place, without inquisitive searching into the ways of the Most High. This must be done for the glory of God's most holy name, and for the lively comfort of his people.

Article 15: *Reprobation*

Moreover, Holy Scripture most especially highlights this eternal and undeserved grace of our election and brings it out more clearly for us, in that it further bears witness that not all people have been chosen but that some have not been chosen or have been passed by in God's eternal election—those, that is, concerning whom God, on the basis of his entirely free, most just, irreproachable, and unchangeable good pleasure, made the following decision:

> to leave them in the common misery into which, by their own fault, they have plunged themselves;

> not to grant them saving faith and the grace of conversion;

> but finally to condemn and eternally punish them (having been left in their own ways and under his just judgment), not only for their unbelief but also for all their other sins, in order to display his justice.

And this is the decision of reprobation, which does not at all make God the author of sin (a blasphemous thought!) but rather its fearful, irreproachable, just judge and avenger.

Article 16: *Responses to the Teaching of Reprobation*
Those who do not yet actively experience within themselves a living faith in Christ or an assured confidence of heart, peace of conscience, a zeal for childlike obedience, and a glorying in God through Christ, but who nevertheless use the means by which God has promised to work these things in us—such people ought not to be alarmed at the mention of reprobation, nor to count themselves among the reprobate; rather they ought to continue diligently in the use of the means, to desire fervently a time of more abundant grace, and to wait for it in reverence and humility. On the other hand, those who seriously desire to turn to God, to be pleasing to him alone, and to be delivered from the body of death, but are not yet able to make such progress along the way of godliness and faith as they would like—such people ought much less to stand in fear of the teaching concerning reprobation, since our merciful God has promised that he will not snuff out a smoldering wick and that he will not break a bruised reed. However, those who have forgotten God and their Savior Jesus Christ and have abandoned themselves wholly to the cares of the world and the pleasures of the flesh—such people have every reason to stand in fear of this teaching, as long as they do not seriously turn to God.

Article 17: *The Salvation of the Infants of Believers*
Since we must make judgments about God's will from his Word, which testifies that the children of believers are holy, not by nature but by virtue of the gracious covenant in which they together with their parents are included, godly parents ought not to doubt the election and salvation of their children whom God calls out of this life in infancy.

Article 18: *The Proper Attitude Toward Election and Reprobation*
To those who complain about this grace of an undeserved election and about the severity of a just reprobation, we reply with the words of the apostle, *Who are you, O man, to talk back to God?* (Rom. 9:20), and with the words of our Savior, *Have I no right to do what I want with my own?* (Matt. 20:15). We, however with reverent adoration of these secret things, cry out with the apostle: *Oh, the depths of the riches both of the wisdom and the knowledge of God! How unsearchable are his judgments, and his ways beyond tracing out! For who has known the mind of the Lord? Or who has been his counselor? Or who has first given to God, that God should repay him? For from him and through him and to him are all things. To him be the glory forever! Amen* (Rom. 11:33–36).

Rejection of the Errors
by Which the Dutch Churches
Have for Some Time Been Disturbed

Having set forth the orthodox teaching concerning election and reprobation, the Synod rejects the errors of those

I

Who teach that the will of God to save those who would believe and persevere in faith and in the obedience of faith is the whole and entire decision of election to salvation, and that nothing else concerning this decision has been revealed in God's Word.

For they deceive the simple and plainly contradict Holy Scripture in its testimony that God does not only wish to save those who would believe, but that he has also from eternity chosen certain particular people to whom, rather than to others, he would within time grant faith in Christ and perseverance. As Scripture says, *I have revealed your name to those whom you gave me* (John 17:6). Likewise, *All who were appointed for eternal life believed* (Acts 13:48), and *He chose us before the foundation of the world so that we should be holy . . .* (Eph. 1:4).

II

Who teach that God's election to eternal life is of many kinds: one general and indefinite, the other particular and definite; and the latter in turn either incomplete, revocable, nonperemptory (or conditional), or else complete, irrevocable, and peremptory (or absolute). Likewise, who teach that there is one election to faith and another to salvation, so that there can be an election to justifying faith apart from a peremptory election to salvation.

For this is an invention of the human brain, devised apart from the Scriptures, which distorts the teaching concerning election and breaks up this golden chain of salvation: *Those whom he predestined, he also called; and those whom he called, he also justified; and those whom he justified, he also glorified* (Rom. 8:30).

III

Who teach that God's good pleasure and purpose, which Scripture mentions in its teaching of election, does not involve God's choosing certain particular people rather than others, but involves God's choosing, out of all possible conditions (including the works of the law) or out of the whole order of things, the intrinsically unworthy act of faith, as well as the imperfect obedience of faith, to be a condition of salvation; and it involves his graciously wishing to count this as perfect obedience and to look upon it as worthy of the reward of eternal life.

For by this pernicious error the good pleasure of God and the merit of Christ are robbed of their effectiveness and people are drawn away, by unprofitable inquiries, from the truth of undeserved justification and from the simplicity of the Scriptures. It also gives the lie to these words of the apostle: *God called us with a holy calling, not in virtue of works, but in virtue of his own purpose and the grace which was given to us in Christ Jesus before the beginning of time* (2 Tim. 1:9).

IV

Who teach that in election to faith a prerequisite condition is that man should rightly use the light of nature, be upright, unassuming, humble, and disposed to eternal life, as though election depended to some extent on these factors.

For this smacks of Pelagius, and it clearly calls into question the words of the apostle: *We lived at one time in the passions of our flesh, following the will of our flesh and thoughts, and we were by nature children of wrath, like everyone else. But God, who is rich in mercy, out of the great love with which he loved us, even when we were dead in transgressions, made us alive with Christ, by whose grace you have been saved. And God raised us up with him and seated us with him in heaven in Christ Jesus, in order that in the coming ages we might show the surpassing riches of his grace, according to his kindness toward us in Christ Jesus. For it*

*is by grace you have been saved, through faith (and this not from
yourselves; it is the gift of God) not by works, so that no one can
boast* (Eph. 2:3–9).

V

Who teach that the incomplete and nonperemptory election of
particular persons to salvation occurred on the basis of a foreseen
faith, repentance, holiness, and godliness, which has just begun
or continued for some time; but that complete and peremptory
election occurred on the basis of a foreseen perseverance to the end
in faith, repentance, holiness, and godliness. And that this is the
gracious and evangelical worthiness, on account of which the one
who is chosen is more worthy than the one who is not chosen. And
therefore that faith, the obedience of faith, holiness, godliness, and
perseverance are not fruits or effects of an unchangeable election
to glory, but indispensable conditions and causes, which are
prerequisite in those who are to be chosen in the complete election,
and which are foreseen as achieved in them.

This runs counter to the entire Scripture, which throughout
impresses upon our ears and hearts these sayings among others:
Election is not by works, but by him who calls (Rom. 9:11–12);
All who were appointed for eternal life believed (Acts 13:48);
He chose us in himself so that we should be holy (Eph. 1:4);
You did not choose me, but I chose you (John 15:16); *If by grace,
not by works* (Rom. 11:6); *In this is love, not that we loved God,
but that he loved us and sent his Son* (1 John 4:10).

VI

Who teach that not every election to salvation is unchangeable, but
that some of the chosen can perish and do in fact perish eternally,
with no decision of God to prevent it.

By this gross error they make God changeable, destroy the comfort
of the godly concerning the steadfastness of their election, and
contradict the Holy Scriptures, which teach that *the elect cannot
be led astray* (Matt. 24:24), *that Christ does not lose those given
to him by the Father* (John 6:39), and that *those whom God
predestined, called, and justified, he also glorifies* (Rom. 8:30).

VII

Who teach that in this life there is no fruit, no awareness, and no assurance of one's unchangeable election to glory, except as conditional upon something changeable and contingent.

For not only is it absurd to speak of an uncertain assurance, but these things also militate against the experience of the saints, who with the apostle rejoice from an awareness of their election and sing the praises of this gift of God; who, as Christ urged, *rejoice* with his disciples *that their names have been written in heaven* (Luke 10:20); and finally who hold up against the flaming arrows of the devil's temptations the awareness of their election, with the question *Who will bring any charge against those whom God has chosen?* (Rom. 8:33).

VIII

Who teach that it was not on the basis of his just will alone that God decided to leave anyone in the fall of Adam and in the common state of sin and condemnation or to pass anyone by in the imparting of grace necessary for faith and conversion.

For these words stand fast: *He has mercy on whom he wishes, and he hardens whom he wishes* (Rom. 9:18). And also: *To you it has been given to know the secrets of the kingdom of heaven, but to them it has not been given* (Matt. 13:11). Likewise: *I give glory to you, Father, Lord of heaven and earth, that you have hidden these things from the wise and understanding, and have revealed them to little children; yes, Father, because that was your pleasure* (Matt. 11:25–26).

IX

Who teach that the cause for God's sending the gospel to one people rather than to another is not merely and solely God's good pleasure, but rather that one people is better and worthier than the other to whom the gospel is not communicated.

For Moses contradicts this when he addresses the people of Israel as follows: *Behold, to Jehovah your God belong the heavens and the highest heavens, the earth and whatever is in it. But Jehovah was inclined in his affection to love your ancestors alone, and chose out their descendants after them, you above all peoples, as at this day* (Deut. 10:14–15). And also Christ: *Woe to you, Korazin! Woe to you, Bethsaida! for if those mighty works done in you had been done in Tyre and Sidon, they would have repented long ago in sackcloth and ashes* (Matt. 11:21).

The Second Main Point of Doctrine
Christ's Death and Human Redemption Through It

Article 1: *The Punishment Which God's Justice Requires*

God is not only supremely merciful, but also supremely just. His justice requires (as he has revealed himself in the Word) that the sins we have committed against his infinite majesty be punished with both temporal and eternal punishments, of soul as well as body. We cannot escape these punishments unless satisfaction is given to God's justice.

Article 2: *The Satisfaction Made by Christ*

Since, however, we ourselves cannot give this satisfaction or deliver ourselves from God's anger, God in his boundless mercy has given us as a guarantee his only begotten Son, who was made to be sin and a curse for us, in our place, on the cross, in order that he might give satisfaction for us.

Article 3: *The Infinite Value of Christ's Death*

This death of God's Son is the only and entirely complete sacrifice and satisfaction for sins; it is of infinite value and worth, more than sufficient to atone for the sins of the whole world.

Article 4: *Reasons for This Infinite Value*

This death is of such great value and worth for the reason that the person who suffered it is—as was necessary to be our Savior—not only a true and perfectly holy man, but also the only begotten Son of God, of the same eternal and infinite essence with the Father and the Holy Spirit. Another reason is that this death was accompanied by the experience of God's anger and curse, which we by our sins had fully deserved.

Article 5: *The Mandate to Proclaim the Gospel to All*

Moreover, it is the promise of the gospel that whoever believes in Christ crucified shall not perish but have eternal life. This promise, together with the command to repent and believe, ought to be announced and declared without differentiation or discrimination to all nations and people, to whom God in his good pleasure sends the gospel.

Article 6: *Unbelief Man's Responsibility*
However, that many who have been called through the gospel do not repent or believe in Christ but perish in unbelief is not because the sacrifice of Christ offered on the cross is deficient or insufficient, but because they themselves are at fault.

Article 7: *Faith God's Gift*
But all who genuinely believe and are delivered and saved by Christ's death from their sins and from destruction receive this favor solely from God's grace—which he owes to no one—given to them in Christ from eternity.

Article 8: *The Saving Effectiveness of Christ's Death*
For it was the entirely free plan and very gracious will and intention of God the Father that the enlivening and saving effectiveness of his Son's costly death should work itself out in all his chosen ones, in order that he might grant justifying faith to them only and thereby lead them without fail to salvation. In other words, it was God's will that Christ through the blood of the cross (by which he confirmed the new covenant) should effectively redeem from every people, tribe, nation, and language all those and only those who were chosen from eternity to salvation and given to him by the Father; that he should grant them faith (which, like the Holy Spirit's other saving gifts, he acquired for them by his death); that he should cleanse them by his blood from all their sins, both original and actual, whether committed before or after their coming to faith; that he should faithfully preserve them to the very end; and that he should finally present them to himself, a glorious people, without spot or wrinkle.

Article 9: *The Fulfillment of God's Plan*
This plan, arising out of God's eternal love for his chosen ones, from the beginning of the world to the present time has been powerfully carried out and will also be carried out in the future, the gates of hell seeking vainly to prevail against it. As a result the chosen are gathered into one, all in their own time, and there is always a church of believers founded on Christ's blood, a church which steadfastly loves, persistently worships, and—here and in all

eternity—praises him as her Savior who laid down his life for her on the cross, as a bridegroom for his bride.

Rejection of Errors

Having set forth the orthodox teaching, the Synod rejects the errors of those

I

Who teach that God the Father appointed his Son to death on the cross without a fixed and definite plan to save anyone by name, so that the necessity, usefulness, and worth of what Christ's death obtained could have stood intact and altogether perfect, complete and whole, even if the redemption that was obtained had never in actual fact been applied to any individual.

For this assertion is an insult to the wisdom of God the Father and to the merit of Jesus Christ, and it is contrary to Scripture. For the Savior speaks as follows: *I lay down my life for the sheep, and I know them* (John 10:15, 27). And Isaiah the prophet says concerning the Savior: *When he shall make himself an offering for sin, he shall see his offspring, he shall prolong his days, and the will of Jehovah shall prosper in his hand* (Isa. 53:10). Finally, this undermines the article of the creed in which we confess what we believe concerning the Church.

II

Who teach that the purpose of Christ's death was not to establish in actual fact a new covenant of grace by his blood, but only to acquire for the Father the mere right to enter once more into a covenant with men, whether of grace or of works.

For this conflicts with Scripture, which teaches that Christ *has become the guarantee and mediator of a better*—that is, *a new—covenant* (Heb. 7:22; 9:15), and that *a will is in force only when someone has died* (Heb. 9:17).

III

Who teach that Christ, by the satisfaction which he gave, did not certainly merit for anyone salvation itself and the faith by which this satisfaction of Christ is effectively applied to salvation, but only acquired for the Father the authority or plenary will to relate in a new way with men and to impose such new conditions as he chose, and that the satisfying of these conditions depends on the free choice of man; consequently, that it was possible that either all or none would fulfill them.

For they have too low an opinion of the death of Christ, do not at all acknowledge the foremost fruit or benefit which it brings forth, and summon back from hell the Pelagian error.

IV

Who teach that what is involved in the new covenant of grace which God the Father made with men through the intervening of Christ's death is not that we are justified before God and saved through faith, insofar as it accepts Christ's merit, but rather that God, having withdrawn his demand for perfect obedience to the law, counts faith itself, and the imperfect obedience of faith, as perfect obedience to the law, and graciously looks upon this as worthy of the reward of eternal life.

For they contradict Scripture: *They are justified freely by his grace through the redemption that came by Jesus Christ, whom God presented as a sacrifice of atonement, through faith in his blood* (Rom. 3:24–25). And along with the ungodly Socinus, they introduce a new and foreign justification of man before God, against the consensus of the whole church.

V

Who teach that all people have been received into the state of reconciliation and into the grace of the covenant, so that no one on account of original sin is liable to condemnation, or is to be condemned, but that all are free from the guilt of this sin.

For this opinion conflicts with Scripture which asserts that we are by nature children of wrath.

VI

Who make use of the distinction between obtaining and applying in order to instill in the unwary and inexperienced the opinion that God, as far as he is concerned, wished to bestow equally upon all people the benefits which are gained by Christ's death; but that the distinction by which some rather than others come to share in the forgiveness of sins and eternal life depends on their own free choice (which applies itself to the grace offered indiscriminately) but does not depend on the unique gift of mercy which effectively works in them, so that they, rather than others, apply that grace to themselves.

For, while pretending to set forth this distinction in an acceptable sense, they attempt to give the people the deadly poison of Pelagianism.

VII

Who teach that Christ neither could die, nor had to die, nor did die for those whom God so dearly loved and chose to eternal life, since such people do not need the death of Christ.

For they contradict the apostle, who says: *Christ loved me and gave himself up for me* (Gal. 2:20), and likewise: *Who will bring any charge against those whom God has chosen? It is God who justifies. Who is he that condemns? It is Christ who died,* that is, for them (Rom. 8:33–34). They also contradict the Savior, who asserts: *I lay down my life for the sheep* (John 10:15), *and My command is this: Love one another as I have loved you, Greater love has no one than this, that one lay down his life for his friends* (John 15:12–13).

The Third and Fourth Main Points of Doctrine
Human Corruption, Conversion to God,
and the Way It Occurs

Article 1: *The Effect of the Fall on Human Nature*

Man was originally created in the image of God and was furnished in his mind with a true and salutary knowledge of his Creator and things spiritual, in his will and heart with righteousness, and in all his emotions with purity; indeed, the whole man was holy. However, rebelling against God at the devil's instigation and by his own free will, he deprived himself of these outstanding gifts. Rather, in their place he brought upon himself blindness, terrible darkness, futility, and distortion of judgment in his mind; perversity, defiance, and hardness in his heart and will; and finally impurity in all his emotions.

Article 2: *The Spread of Corruption*

Man brought forth children of the same nature as himself after the fall. That is to say, being corrupt he brought forth corrupt children. The corruption spread, by God's just judgment, from Adam to all his descendants—except for Christ alone—not by way of imitation (as in former times the Pelagians would have it) but by way of the propagation of his perverted nature.

Article 3: *Total Inability*

Therefore, all people are conceived in sin and are born children of wrath, unfit for any saving good, inclined to evil, dead in their sins, and slaves to sin; without the grace of the regenerating Holy Spirit they are neither willing nor able to return to God, to reform their distorted nature, or even to dispose themselves to such reform.

Article 4: *The Inadequacy of the Light of Nature*

There is, to be sure, a certain light of nature remaining in man after the fall, by virtue of which he retains some notions about God, natural things, and the difference between what is moral and immoral, and demonstrates a certain eagerness for virtue and for good outward behavior. But this light of nature is far from enabling man to come to a saving knowledge of God and conversion to him—so far, in fact, that man does not use it rightly even in matters of nature and society. Instead, in various ways he completely distorts this light, whatever its precise character, and suppresses it in unrighteousness. In doing so he renders himself without excuse before God.

Article 5: *The Inadequacy of the Law*
In this respect, what is true of the light of nature is true also of the Ten Commandments given by God through Moses specifically to the Jews. For man cannot obtain saving grace through the Decalogue, because, although it does expose the magnitude of his sin and increasingly convict him of his guilt, yet it does not offer a remedy or enable him to escape from his misery, and, indeed, weakened as it is by the flesh, leaves the offender under the curse.

Article 6: *The Saving Power of the Gospel*
What, therefore, neither the light of nature nor the law can do, God accomplishes by the power of the Holy Spirit, through the Word or the ministry of reconciliation. This is the gospel about the Messiah, through which it has pleased God to save believers, in both the Old and the New Testament.

Article 7: *God's Freedom in Revealing the Gospel*
In the Old Testament, God revealed this secret of his will to a small number; in the New Testament (now without any distinction between peoples) he discloses it to a large number. The reason for this difference must not be ascribed to the greater worth of one nation over another, or to a better use of the light of nature, but to the free good pleasure and undeserved love of God. Therefore, those who receive so much grace, beyond and in spite of all they deserve, ought to acknowledge it with humble and thankful hearts; on the other hand, with the apostle they ought to adore (but certainly not inquisitively search into) the severity and justice of God's judgments on the others, who do not receive this grace.

Article 8: *The Serious Call of the Gospel*
Nevertheless, all who are called through the gospel are called seriously. For seriously and most genuinely God makes known in his Word what is pleasing to him: that those who are called should

come to him. Seriously he also promises rest for their souls and eternal life to all who come to him and believe.

Article 9: *Human Responsibility for Rejecting the Gospel*
The fact that many who are called through the ministry of the gospel do not come and are not brought to conversion must not be blamed on the gospel, nor on Christ, who is offered through the gospel, nor on God, who calls them through the gospel and even bestows various gifts on them, but on the people themselves who are called. Some in self-assurance do not even entertain the Word of life; others do entertain it but do not take it to heart, and for that reason, after the fleeting joy of a temporary faith, they relapse; others choke the seed of the Word with the thorns of life's cares and with the pleasures of the world and bring forth no fruits. This our Savior teaches in the parable of the sower (Matt. 13).

Article 10: *Conversion as the Work of God*
The fact that others who are called through the ministry of the gospel do come and are brought to conversion must not be credited to man, as though one distinguishes himself by free choice from others who are furnished with equal or sufficient grace for faith and conversion (as the proud heresy of Pelagius maintains). No, it must be credited to God: just as from eternity he chose his own in Christ, so within time he effectively calls them, grants them faith and repentance, and having rescued them from the dominion of darkness, brings them into the kingdom of his Son, in order that they may declare the wonderful deeds of him who called them out of darkness into this marvelous light, and may boast not in themselves, but in the Lord, as apostolic words frequently testify in Scripture.

Article 11: *The Holy Spirit's Work in Conversion*
Moreover, when God carries out this good pleasure in his chosen ones, or works true conversion in them, he not only sees to it that the gospel is proclaimed to them outwardly, and enlightens their minds powerfully by the Holy Spirit so that they may rightly understand and discern the things of the Spirit of God, but, by the effective operation of the same regenerating Spirit, he also penetrates into

the inmost being of man, opens the closed heart, softens the hard heart, and circumcises the heart that is uncircumcised. He infuses new qualities into the will, making the dead will alive, the evil one good, the unwilling one willing, and the stubborn one compliant; he activates and strengthens the will so that, like a good tree, it may be enabled to produce the fruits of good deeds.

Article 12: *Regeneration a Supernatural Work*

And this is the regeneration, the new creation, the raising from the dead, and the making alive so clearly proclaimed in the Scriptures, which God works in us without our help. But this certainly does not happen only by outward teaching, by moral persuasion, or by such a way of working that, after God has done his work, it remains in man's power whether or not to be reborn or converted. Rather, it is an entirely supernatural work, one that is at the same time most powerful and most pleasing, a marvelous, hidden, and inexpressible work, which is not lesser than or inferior in power to that of creation or of raising the dead, as Scripture (inspired by the author of this work) teaches. As a result, all those in whose hearts God works in this marvelous way are certainly, unfailingly, and effectively reborn and do actually believe. And then the will, now renewed, is not only activated and motivated by God, but in being activated by God is also itself active. For this reason, man himself, by that grace which he has received, is also rightly said to believe and to repent.

Article 13: *The Incomprehensible Way of Regeneration*

In this life believers cannot fully understand the way this work occurs; meanwhile, they rest content with knowing and experiencing that by this grace of God they do believe with the heart and love their Savior.

Article 14: *The Way God Gives Faith*

In this way, therefore, faith is a gift of God, not in the sense that it is offered by God for man to choose, but that it is in actual fact bestowed on man, breathed and infused into him. Nor is it a gift in the sense that God bestows only the potential to believe, but then awaits assent—the act of believing—from man's choice; rather, it is a gift in the sense that he who works both willing and acting and, indeed, works all things in all people produces in man both the will to believe and the belief itself.

Article 15: *Responses to God's Grace*
God does not owe this grace to anyone. For what could God owe to one who has nothing to give that can be paid back? Indeed, what could God owe to one who has nothing of his own to give but sin and falsehood? Therefore the person who receives this grace owes and gives eternal thanks to God alone; the person who does not receive it either does not care at all about these spiritual things and is satisfied with himself in his condition, or else in self-assurance foolishly boasts about having something which he lacks. Furthermore, following the example of the apostles, we are to think and to speak in the most favorable way about those who outwardly profess their faith and better their lives, for the inner chambers of the heart are unknown to us. But for others who have not yet been called, we are to pray to the God who calls things that do not exist as though they did. In no way, however, are we to pride ourselves as better than they, as though we had distinguished ourselves from them.

Article 16: *Regeneration's Effect*
However, just as by the fall man did not cease to be man, endowed with intellect and will, and just as sin, which has spread through the whole human race, did not abolish the nature of the human race but distorted and spiritually killed it, so also this divine grace of regeneration does not act in people as if they were blocks and stones; nor does it abolish the will and its properties or coerce a reluctant will by force, but spiritually revives, heals, reforms, and—in a manner at once pleasing and powerful—bends it back. As a result, a ready and sincere obedience of the Spirit now begins to prevail where before the rebellion and resistance of the flesh were completely dominant. It is in this that the true and spiritual restoration and freedom of our will consists. Thus, if the marvelous Maker of every good thing were not dealing with us, man would have no hope of getting up from his fall by his free choice, by which he plunged himself into ruin when still standing upright.

Article 17: *God's Use of Means in Regeneration*
Just as the almighty work of God by which he brings forth
and sustains our natural life does not rule out but requires the
use of means, by which God, according to his infinite wisdom
and goodness, has wished to exercise his power, so also the
aforementioned supernatural work of God by which he regenerates
us in no way rules out or cancels the use of the gospel, which God in
his great wisdom has appointed to be the seed of regeneration and
the food of the soul. For this reason, the apostles and the teachers
who followed them taught the people in a godly manner about this
grace of God, to give him the glory and to humble all pride, and
yet did not neglect meanwhile to keep the people, by means of the
holy admonitions of the gospel, under the administration of the
Word, the sacraments, and discipline. So even today it is out of
the question that the teachers or those taught in the church should
presume to test God by separating what he in his good pleasure has
wished to be closely joined together. For grace is bestowed through
admonitions, and the more readily we perform our duty, the more
lustrous the benefit of God working in us usually is and the better
his work advances. To him alone, both for the means and for their
saving fruit and effectiveness, all glory is owed forever. Amen.

Rejection of Errors

Having set forth the orthodox teaching, the Synod rejects the
errors of those

I

Who teach that, properly speaking, it cannot be said that original
sin in itself is enough to condemn the whole human race or to
warrant temporal and eternal punishments.

For they contradict the apostle when he says: *Sin entered the
world through one man, and death through sin, and in this way
death passed on to all men because all sinned* (Rom. 5:12); also:
The guilt followed one sin and brought condemnation
(Rom. 5:16); likewise: *The wages of sin is death* (Rom. 6:23).

II

Who teach that the spiritual gifts or the good dispositions and virtues such as goodness, holiness, and righteousness could not have resided in man's will when he was first created, and therefore could not have been separated from the will at the fall.

For this conflicts with the apostle's description of the image of God in Ephesians 4:24, where he portrays the image in terms of righteousness and holiness, which definitely reside in the will.

III

Who teach that in spiritual death the spiritual gifts have not been separated from man's will, since the will in itself has never been corrupted but only hindered by the darkness of the mind and the unruliness of the emotions, and since the will is able to exercise its innate free capacity once these hindrances are removed, which is to say, it is able of itself to will or choose whatever good is set before it—or else not to will or choose it.

This is a novel idea and an error and has the effect of elevating the power of free choice, contrary to the words of Jeremiah the prophet: *The heart itself is deceitful above all things and wicked* (Jer. 17:9); and of the words of the apostle: *All of us also lived among them* (the sons of disobedience) *at one time in the passions of our flesh, following the will of our flesh and thoughts* (Eph. 2:3).

IV

Who teach that unregenerate man is not strictly or totally dead in his sins or deprived of all capacity for spiritual good but is able to hunger and thirst for righteousness or life and to offer the sacrifice of a broken and contrite spirit which is pleasing to God.

For these views are opposed to the plain testimonies of Scripture: *You were dead in your transgressions and sins* (Eph. 2:1,5); *The imagination of the thoughts of man's heart is only evil all the time* (Gen. 6:5; 8:21). Besides, to hunger and thirst for deliverance from misery and for life, and to offer God the sacrifice of a broken spirit is characteristic only of the regenerate and of those called blessed (Ps. 51:17; Matt. 5:6).

V

Who teach that corrupt and natural man can make such good use of common grace (by which they mean the light of nature) or of the gifts remaining after the fall that he is able thereby gradually to obtain a greater grace—evangelical or saving grace—as well as salvation itself; and that in this way God, for his part, shows himself ready to reveal Christ to all people, since he provides to all to a sufficient extent and in an effective manner, the means necessary for the revealing of Christ, for faith, and for repentance. For Scripture, not to mention the experience of all ages, testifies that this is false: *He makes known his words to Jacob, his statutes and his laws to Israel; he has done this for no other nation, and they do not know his laws* (Ps. 147:19–20); *In the past God let all nations go their own way* (Acts 14:16); *They* (Paul and his companions) *were kept by the Holy Spirit from speaking God's word in Asia; and When they had come to Mysia, they tried to go to Bithynia, but the Spirit would not allow them to* (Acts 16:6–7).

VI

Who teach that in the true conversion of man new qualities, dispositions, or gifts cannot be infused or poured into his will by God, and indeed that the faith [or believing] by which we first come to conversion and from which we receive the name "believers" is not a quality or gift infused by God, but only an act of man, and that it cannot be called a gift except in respect to the power of attaining faith.

For these views contradict the Holy Scriptures, which testify that God does infuse or pour into our hearts the new qualities of faith, obedience, and the experiencing of his love: *I will put my law in their minds, and write it on their hearts* (Jer. 31:33); *I will pour water on the thirsty land, and streams on the dry ground; I will pour out my Spirit on your offspring* (Isa. 44:3); *The love of God has been poured out in our hearts by the Holy Spirit, who has been given to us* (Rom. 5:5). They also conflict with the continuous practice of the Church, which prays with the prophet: *Convert me, Lord, and I shall be converted* (Jer. 31:18).

VII

Who teach that the grace by which we are converted to God is nothing but a gentle persuasion, or (as others explain it) that the way of God's acting in man's conversion that is most noble and suited to human nature is that which happens by persuasion, and that nothing prevents this grace of moral suasion even by itself from making natural men spiritual; indeed, that God does not produce the assent of the will except in this manner of moral suasion, and that the effectiveness of God's work by which it surpasses the work of Satan consists in the fact that God promises eternal benefits while Satan promises temporal ones.

For this teaching is entirely Pelagian and contrary to the whole of Scripture, which recognizes besides this persuasion also another, far more effective and divine way in which the Holy Spirit acts in man's conversion. As Ezekiel 36:26 puts it: *I will give you a new heart and put a new spirit in you; and I will remove your heart of stone and give you a heart of flesh . . . .*

VIII

Who teach that God in regenerating man does not bring to bear that power of his omnipotence whereby he may powerfully and unfailingly bend man's will to faith and conversion, but that even when God has accomplished all the works of grace which he uses for man's conversion, man nevertheless can, and in actual fact often does, so resist God and the Spirit in their intent and will to regenerate him, that man completely thwarts his own rebirth; and, indeed, that it remains in his own power whether or not to be reborn.

For this does away with all effective functioning of God's grace in our conversion and subjects the activity of Almighty God to the will of man; it is contrary to the apostles, who teach that *we believe by virtue of the effective working of God's mighty strength* (Eph. 1:19), and that *God fulfills the undeserved good will of his kindness and the work of faith in us with power* (2 Thess. 1:11), and likewise that *his divine power has given us everything we need for life and godliness* (2 Pet. 1:3).

IX

Who teach that grace and free choice are concurrent partial causes which cooperate to initiate conversion, and that grace does not precede—in the order of causality—the effective influence of the will; that is to say, that God does not effectively help man's will to come to conversion before man's will itself motivates and determines itself.

For the early church already condemned this doctrine long ago in the Pelagians, on the basis of the words of the apostle: *It does not depend on man's willing or running but on God's mercy* (Rom. 9:16); also: *Who makes you different from anyone else?* and *What do you have that you did not receive?* (1 Cor. 4:7); likewise: *It is God who works in you to will and act according to his good pleasure* (Phil. 2:13).

The Fifth Main Point of Doctrine
The Perseverance of the Saints

Article 1: *The Regenerate Not Entirely Free from Sin*
Those people whom God according to his purpose calls into fellowship with his Son Jesus Christ our Lord and regenerates by the Holy Spirit, he also sets free from the reign and slavery of sin, though in this life not entirely from the flesh and from the body of sin.

Article 2: *The Believer's Reaction to Sins of Weakness*
Hence daily sins of weakness arise, and blemishes cling to even the best works of God's people, giving them continual cause to humble themselves before God, to flee for refuge to Christ crucified, to put the flesh to death more and more by the Spirit of supplication and by holy exercises of godliness, and to strain toward the goal of perfection, until they are freed from this body of death and reign with the Lamb of God in heaven.

Article 3: *God's Preservation of the Converted*
Because of these remnants of sin dwelling in them and also because of the temptations of the world and Satan, those who have been converted could not remain standing in this grace if left to their own resources. But God is faithful, mercifully strengthening them in the grace once conferred on them and powerfully preserving them in it to the end.

Article 4: *The Danger of True Believers' Falling into Serious Sins*
Although that power of God strengthening and preserving true believers in grace is more than a match for the flesh, yet those converted are not always so activated and motivated by God that in certain specific actions they cannot by their own fault depart from the leading of grace, be led astray by the desires of the flesh, and give in to them. For this reason they must constantly watch and pray that they may not be led into temptations. When they fail to do this, not only can they be carried away by the flesh, the world, and Satan into sins, even serious and outrageous ones, but also by God's just permission they sometimes are so carried away—

witness the sad cases, described in Scripture, of David, Peter, and other saints falling into sins.

Article 5: *The Effects of Such Serious Sins*

By such monstrous sins, however, they greatly offend God, deserve the sentence of death, grieve the Holy Spirit, suspend the exercise of faith, severely wound the conscience, and sometimes lose the awareness of grace for a time—until, after they have returned to the way by genuine repentance, God's fatherly face again shines upon them.

Article 6: *God's Saving Intervention*

For God, who is rich in mercy, according to his unchangeable purpose of election does not take his Holy Spirit from his own completely, even when they fall grievously. Neither does he let them fall down so far that they forfeit the grace of adoption and the state of justification, or commit the sin which leads to death (the sin against the Holy Spirit), and plunge themselves, entirely forsaken by him, into eternal ruin.

Article 7: *Renewal to Repentance*

For, in the first place, God preserves in those saints when they fall his imperishable seed from which they have been born again, lest it perish or be dislodged. Secondly, by his Word and Spirit he certainly and effectively renews them to repentance so that they have a heartfelt and godly sorrow for the sins they have committed; seek and obtain, through faith and with a contrite heart, forgiveness in the blood of the Mediator; experience again the grace of a reconciled God; through faith adore his mercies; and from then on more eagerly work out their own salvation with fear and trembling.

Article 8: *The Certainty of This Preservation*

So it is not by their own merits or strength but by God's undeserved mercy that they neither forfeit faith and grace totally nor remain in their downfalls to the end and are lost. With respect to themselves this not only easily could happen, but also undoubtedly would happen; but with respect to God it cannot possibly happen, since his plan cannot be changed, his promise cannot fail, the calling according to his purpose cannot be revoked, the merit of Christ as well as his interceding and preserving cannot be nullified, and the sealing of the Holy Spirit can neither be invalidated nor wiped out.

Article 9: *The Assurance of This Preservation*
Concerning this preservation of those chosen to salvation and concerning the perseverance of true believers in faith, believers themselves can and do become assured in accordance with the measure of their faith, by which they firmly believe that they are and always will remain true and living members of the church, and that they have the forgiveness of sins and eternal life.

Article 10: *The Ground of This Assurance*
Accordingly, this assurance does not derive from some private revelation beyond or outside the Word, but from faith in the promises of God which he has very plentifully revealed in his Word for our comfort, from the testimony of *the Holy Spirit testifying with our spirit that we are God's children and heirs* (Rom. 8:16–17), and finally from a serious and holy pursuit of a clear conscience and of good works. And if God's chosen ones in this world did not have this well-founded comfort that the victory will be theirs and this reliable guarantee of eternal glory, they would be of all people most miserable.

Article 11: *Doubts Concerning This Assurance*
Meanwhile, Scripture testifies that believers have to contend in this life with various doubts of the flesh and that under severe temptation they do not always experience this full assurance of faith and certainty of perseverance. But God, the Father of all comfort, *does not let them be tempted beyond what they can bear, but with the temptation he also provides a way out* (1 Cor. 10:13), and by the Holy Spirit revives in them the assurance of their perseverance.

Article 12: *This Assurance as an Incentive to Godliness*
This assurance of perseverance, however, so far from making true believers proud and carnally self-assured, is rather the true root of humility, of childlike respect, of genuine godliness, of endurance in every conflict, of fervent prayers, of steadfastness in crossbearing

and in confessing the truth, and of well-founded joy in God. Reflecting on this benefit provides an incentive to a serious and continual practice of thanksgiving and good works, as is evident from the testimonies of Scripture and the examples of the saints.

Article 13: *Assurance No Inducement to Carelessness*
Neither does the renewed confidence of perseverance produce immorality or lack of concern for godliness in those put back on their feet after a fall, but it produces a much greater concern to observe carefully the ways of the Lord which he prepared in advance. They observe these ways in order that by walking in them they may maintain the assurance of their perseverance, lest, by their abuse of his fatherly goodness, the face of the gracious God (for the godly, looking upon his face is sweeter than life, but its withdrawal is more bitter than death) turn away from them again, with the result that they fall into greater anguish of spirit.

Article 14: *God's Use of Means in Perseverance*
And, just as it has pleased God to begin this work of grace in us by the proclamation of the gospel, so he preserves, continues, and completes his work by the hearing and reading of the gospel, by meditation on it, by its exhortations, threats, and promises, and also by the use of the sacraments.

Article 15: *Contrasting Reactions to the Teaching of Perseverance*
This teaching about the perseverance of true believers and saints, and about their assurance of it—a teaching which God has very richly revealed in his Word for the glory of his name and for the comfort of the godly and which he impresses on the hearts of believers—is something which the flesh does not understand, Satan hates, the world ridicules, the ignorant and the hypocrites abuse, and the spirits of error attack. The bride of Christ, on the other hand, has always loved this teaching very tenderly and defended it steadfastly as a priceless treasure; and God, against whom no plan can avail and no strength can prevail, will ensure that she will continue to do this. To this God alone, Father, Son, and Holy Spirit, be honor and glory forever. Amen.

Rejection of the Errors
Concerning the Teaching of
the Perseverance of the Saints

Having set forth the orthodox teaching, the Synod rejects the errors of those

I

Who teach that the perseverance of true believers is not an effect of election or a gift of God produced by Christ's death, but a condition of the new covenant which man, before what they call his "peremptory" election and justification, must fulfill by his free will.

For Holy Scripture testifies that perseverance follows from election and is granted to the chosen by virtue of Christ's death, resurrection, and intercession: *The chosen obtained it; the others were hardened* (Rom. 11:7); likewise, *He who did not spare his own son, but gave him up for us all—how will he not, along with him, grant us all things? Who will bring any charge against those whom God has chosen? It is God who justifies. Who is he that condemns? It is Christ Jesus who died—more than that, who was raised—who also sits at the right hand of God, and is also interceding for us. Who shall separate us from the love of Christ?* (Rom. 8:32–35).

II

Who teach that God does provide the believer with sufficient strength to persevere and is ready to preserve this strength in him if he performs his duty, but that even with all those things in place which are necessary to persevere in faith and which God is pleased to use to preserve faith, it still always depends on the choice of man's will whether or not he perseveres.

For this view is obviously Pelagian; and though it intends to make men free it makes them sacrilegious. It is against the enduring consensus of evangelical teaching which takes from man all cause for boasting and ascribes the praise for this benefit only to God's grace. It is also against the testimony of the apostle: *It is God who keeps us strong to the end, so that we will be blameless on the day of our Lord Jesus Christ* (1 Cor. 1:8).

III

Who teach that those who truly believe and have been born again not only can forfeit justifying faith as well as grace and salvation totally and to the end, but also in actual fact do often forfeit them and are lost forever.

For this opinion nullifies the very grace of justification and regeneration as well as the continual preservation by Christ, contrary to the plain words of the apostle Paul: *If Christ died for us while we were still sinners, we will therefore much more be saved from God's wrath through him, since we have now been justified by his blood* (Rom. 5:8–9); and contrary to the apostle John: *No one who is born of God is intent on sin, because God's seed remains in him, nor can he sin, because he has been born of God* (1 John 3:9); also contrary to the words of Jesus Christ: *I give eternal life to my sheep, and they shall never perish; no one can snatch them out of my hand. My Father, who has given them to me, is greater than all; no one can snatch them out of my Father's hand* (John 10:28–29).

IV

Who teach that those who truly believe and have been born again can commit the sin that leads to death (the sin against the Holy Spirit).

For the same apostle John, after making mention of those who commit the sin that leads to death and forbidding prayer for them (1 John 5:16–17), immediately adds: *We know that anyone born of God does not commit sin* (that is, that kind of sin), *but the one who was born of God keeps himself safe, and the evil one does not touch him* (v.18).

V

Who teach that apart from a special revelation no one can have the assurance of future perseverance in this life.

For by this teaching the well-founded consolation of true believers in this life is taken away and the doubting of the Romanists is reintroduced into the church. Holy Scripture, however, in many places derives the assurance not from a special and extraordinary revelation but from the marks peculiar to God's children and from God's completely reliable promises. So especially the apostle Paul: *Nothing in all creation can separate us from the love of God that is in Christ Jesus our Lord* (Rom. 8:39); and John: *They who obey his commands remain in him and he in them. And this is how we know that he remains in us: by the Spirit he gave us* (1 John 3:24).

VI

Who teach that the teaching of the assurance of perseverance and of salvation is by its very nature and character an opiate of the flesh and is harmful to godliness, good morals, prayer, and other holy exercises, but that, on the contrary, to have doubt about this is praiseworthy.

For these people show that they do not know the effective operation of God's grace and the work of the indwelling Holy Spirit, and they contradict the apostle John, who asserts the opposite in plain words: *Dear friends, now we are children of God, but what we will be has not yet been made known. But we know that when he is made known, we shall be like him, for we shall see him as he is. Everyone who has this hope in him purifies himself, just as he is pure* (1 John 3:2–3). Moreover, they are refuted by the examples of the saints in both the Old and the New Testament, who though assured of their perseverance and salvation yet were constant in prayer and other exercises of godliness.

VII

Who teach that the faith of those who believe only temporarily does not differ from justifying and saving faith except in duration alone.

For Christ himself in Matthew 13:20ff. and Luke 8:13ff. clearly defines these further differences between temporary and true believers: he says that the former receive the seed on rocky ground, and the latter receive it in good ground, or a good heart; the former have no root, and the latter are firmly rooted; the former have no fruit, and the latter produce fruit in varying measure, with steadfastness, or perseverance.

VIII

Who teach that it is not absurd that a person, after losing his former regeneration, should once again, indeed quite often, be reborn.

For by this teaching they deny the imperishable nature of God's seed by which we are born again, contrary to the testimony of the apostle Peter: *Born again, not of perishable seed, but of imperishable* (1 Pet. 1:23).

IX

Who teach that Christ nowhere prayed for an unfailing perseverance of believers in faith.

For they contradict Christ himself when he says: *I have prayed for you, Peter, that your faith may not fail* (Luke 22:32); and John the gospel writer when he testifies in John 17 that it was not only for the apostles, but also for all those who were to believe by their message that Christ prayed: *Holy Father, preserve them in your name* (v. 11); and *My prayer is not that you take them out of the world, but that you preserve them from the evil one* (v.15).

Conclusion

Rejection of False Accusations

And so this is the clear, simple, and straightforward explanation of the orthodox teaching on the five articles in dispute in the Netherlands, as well as the rejection of the errors by which the Dutch churches have for some time been disturbed. This explanation and rejection the Synod declares to be derived from God's Word and in agreement with the confessions of the Reformed churches. Hence it clearly appears that those of whom one could hardly expect it have shown no truth, equity, and charity at all in wishing to make the public believe:

> —that the teaching of the Reformed churches on predestination and on the points associated with it by its very nature and tendency draws the minds of people away from all godliness and religion, is an opiate of the flesh and the

devil, and is a stronghold of Satan where he lies in wait for all people, wounds most of them, and fatally pierces many of them with the arrows of both despair and self-assurance;

—that this teaching makes God the author of sin, unjust, a tyrant, and a hypocrite; and is nothing but a refurbished Stoicism, Manicheism, Libertinism, and Mohammedanism;

—that this teaching makes people carnally self-assured, since it persuades them that nothing endangers the salvation of the chosen, no matter how they live, so that they may commit the most outrageous crimes with self-assurance; and that on the other hand nothing is of use to the reprobate for salvation even if they have truly performed all the works of the saints;

—that this teaching means that God predestined and created, by the bare and unqualified choice of his will, without the least regard or consideration of any sin, the greatest part of the world to eternal condemnation; that in the same manner in which election is the source and cause of faith and good works, reprobation is the cause of unbelief and ungodliness; that many infant children of believers are snatched in their innocence from their mothers' breasts and cruelly cast into hell so that neither the blood of Christ nor their baptism nor the prayers of the church at their baptism can be of any use to them;

and very many other slanderous accusations of this kind which the Reformed churches not only disavow but even denounce with their whole heart.

Therefore this Synod of Dort in the name of the Lord pleads with all who devoutly call on the name of our Savior Jesus Christ to form their judgment about the faith of the Reformed churches, not on the basis of false accusations gathered from here or there, or even on the basis of the personal statements of a number of ancient and modern authorities—statements which are also often either quoted out of context or misquoted and twisted to convey a different meaning—but on the basis of the churches' own official confessions and of the present explanation of the orthodox teaching which has been endorsed by the unanimous consent of the members of the whole Synod, one and all.

Moreover, the Synod earnestly warns the false accusers themselves to consider how heavy a judgment of God awaits those who give false testimony against so many churches and their confessions, trouble the consciences of the weak, and seek to prejudice the minds of many against the fellowship of true believers.

Finally, this Synod urges all fellow ministers in the gospel of Christ to deal with this teaching in a godly and reverent manner, in the academic institutions as well as in the churches; to do so, both in their speaking and writing, with a view to the glory of God's name, holiness of life, and the comfort of anxious souls; to think and also speak with Scripture according to the analogy of faith; and, finally, to refrain from all those ways of speaking which go beyond the bounds set for us by the genuine sense of the Holy Scriptures and which could give impertinent sophists a just occasion to scoff at the teaching of the Reformed churches or even to bring false accusations against it.

May God's Son Jesus Christ, who sits at the right hand of God and gives gifts to men, sanctify us in the truth, lead to the truth those who err, silence the mouths of those who lay false accusations against sound teaching, and equip faithful ministers of his Word with a spirit of wisdom and discretion, that all they say may be to the glory of God and the building up of their hearers. Amen.

Note to the Reader

The publisher invites you to respond to us about this book by writing to Reformed Fellowship, Inc., at *president@ reformedfellowship.net*

Founded in 1951, Reformed Fellowship, Inc., is a religious and strictly nonprofit organization composed of a group of Christian believers who hold to the biblical Reformed faith. Our purpose is to advocate and propagate this faith, to nurture those who seek to live in obedience to it, to give sharpened expression to it, to stimulate the doctrinal sensitivities of those who profess it, to promote the spiritual welfare and purity of the Reformed churches, and to encourage Christian action.

Members of Reformed Fellowship express their adherence to the Calvinistic creeds as formulated in the *Belgic Confession*, the *Heidelberg Catechism*, the *Canons of Dort*, and the *Westminster Confession and Catechisms*.

To fulfill our mission, we publish a bimonthly journal, *The Outlook*, and we publish books and Bible study guides. Our website is *www.reformedfellowship.net*